⊠   *The Nakedness of the Fathers*   ⊠

The Nakedness of the Fathers

BIBLICAL VISIONS AND REVISIONS

BY

Alicia Suskin Ostriker

Rutgers University Press
New Brunswick, New Jersey

Library of Congress Cataloging-in-Publication Data
Ostriker, Suskin Alicia.

The nakedness of the Fathers : biblical visions and revisions / by
Alicia Suskin Ostriker.

    p. cm.

Includes bibliographical references.

    1. Bible and feminism.   2. Bible and literature.   3. Feminism—
Religious aspects—Judaism.   4. Bible. O.T.—Criticism, interpretation,
etc.   I. Title

BS680.W7088   1994   94-14616
221.6'082—dc   CIP

*Grateful acknowledgment is made to the following books and journals in which
portions of this book have previously appeared, sometimes in earlier versions:*

Feminist Studies: "Entering the Tents"

Fiction: "The Wrestling"

Iowa Review: "Job, or a Meditation on Justice"

Kenyon Review: "The Wisdom of Solomon," "Esther, or the World Turned
    Upside Down," "The Interpretation of Dreams"

Lilith: "Survival," "The Story of Joshua"

Michigan Quarterly Review: "The Garden"

Ontario Review: "The Cave," "Cain and Abel: A Question in Ethics"

Out of the Garden: "The Nursing Father" is reprinted with the permission of
    Ballantine Books

Reading Ruth: "The Redeeming of Ruth" is printed here with the permission
    of Ballantine Books

Santa Monica Review: "Intensive Care"

Studies in American Jewish Literature: "A Prayer to the Shekhinah" and
    "The Redeeming of Ruth" are reprinted with the permission of The Kent
    State University Press

Thirteenth Moon: "Rebecca's Way," "Rachel and Leah: A Question of
    Rivalry," "The Songs of Miriam," "The Opinion of Aaron"

Tikkun: "The Passion of Sarah" and "The Opinion of Hagar" appeared in
    earlier versions in TIKKUN, A BI-MONTHLY JEWISH CRITIQUE OF POLITICS,
    CULTURE, AND SOCIETY. 251 West 100th Street, 5th floor, New York, NY 10025

*This book is dedicated
with gratitude
to my father,
David Suskin,
and to my grandfathers,
Simon Linnick and Harry Suskin*

*To pursue peace is equal
to all the commandments of Torah*

"*It shall come to pass afterward that I will pour out my spirit upon all flesh; and your sons and daughters shall prophesy, your old men shall dream dreams, and your young men shall see visions; and also upon the servants and the handmaids . . . will I pour out my spirit.*"

JOEL 2:28–29

Contents

✥ *Preface* ✥

*"Not with our ancestors did God make this
covenant, but with us, who are all of us here alive
this day."*
DEUTERONOMY 5:3

Some years ago I came home from work on a stormy night,
took off my wet things, picked up a notebook and pen, and
started to jot down some thoughts about the Book of Job. I had
no particular purpose in mind. I had not especially planned to
do any writing on this subject. The general idea was that the
God of what Christians call the Old Testament and Jews call,
simply, the Bible or Torah, seems to like being challenged and
called to account, and even rewards those who most boldly
interrogate him. As I puzzled over the paradoxical dialogue
between Job and God, in which Job's challenge to God's justice
is first scorned, then affirmed, my thoughts were at first recog-
nizably my own. Then something happened. I found myself
writing, without forethought and at astonishing speed, as if
someone else were directing the pen, about Job's wife, that
nameless woman. How would Job's wife feel about having the
ten children who had been casually slain in order to test her
husband's devotion to his God, replaced by ten new children?
And what if Job's wife were to get up the courage to challenge
God like her husband? What would she—what would we—say
to God if we dared? By the time my pen stopped, I understood

that I was on a train I could not get off. *The Nakedness of the Fathers* is the result.

As the writing has gradually unfolded I have been repeatedly astonished by the degree to which the Bible exceeds the doctrines that have been built upon it. Again and again I remember Solomon's confession to God: "Behold, the heaven of heavens cannot contain thee; how much less this house which I have builded." The Bible, it should be evident to anyone who reads with open eyes, is an endlessly complex, provocative, layered, contradictory set of documents, as befits its composition over a period of millennia during which the very conception of God was changing. Scripture harbors within its boundaries a record of living spiritual experiences from countless sources, including half-erased traces of paganism and bold borrowings from Hellenic philosophy; acts of interpretation and re-interpretation are already part of its fabric. Rabbinic tradition itself tells us to expect that the process of understanding the Bible's meaning will and should continue throughout history. According to the sages, all commentary on Torah—past, present, future— was implicitly part of the revelation at Sinai. As the scholar Gerald Bruns has argued, "if the text does not apply to us it is an empty text. . . . We take the text in relation to ourselves, understanding ourselves in its light, even as our situation throws its light upon the text, allowing it to disclose itself differently, perhaps in unheard-of ways."[†]

Throughout the history of the Diaspora, Jewish imagination has flowered through midrash—stories based on Biblical stories, composed not for a narrow audience of scholars, but for

---

[†] Gerald L. Bruns, "Midrash and Allegory: The Beginning of Scriptural Interpretation," in *The Literary Guide to the Bible*, ed. Robert Alter and Frank Kermode (Cambridge, Mass.: Harvard University Press, 1987), 633.

an entire community. It is this tradition to which I hope to belong. In midrash, ancient tales yield new meanings to new generations. Not surprisingly, many midrashists today are women; we should expect many more in the future. How could it be otherwise? The texts plainly beg and implore women to read them as freshly, energetically, passionately—and even playfully—as they have been read by men. "Turn it and turn it," the rabbis say of Torah, "for everything is in it." Besides, they tell us, God has intended "all the meanings that He has made us capable of discovering." If so, the truths of women are present in this text, sacred comedy as well as sacred tragedy, but we will not see these truths until women do their own reading, perform their own acts of discovery. By the time the spiritual imagination of women has expressed itself as fully and variously as that of men, to be sure, whatever humanity means by God, religion, holiness, and truth will be completely transformed.

❧

When I began this book, the work seemed frighteningly solitary. It has since become communal. To know that the task is a collective one is deeply comforting. I have drawn upon the aid of numberless others, including friends, colleagues, and students who heroically read the manuscript at various stages, who peppered me with questions, objections, suggestions, and amplifications, and who offered affirmations of the project which made it possible to go on writing. I am especially indebted to Sheila Solomon, Shirley Kaufman Daleski, Eleanor Wilner, Susan Stanford Friedman, Lori Lefkowitz, Leonard Gordon, Ruth Yeselson, Celia Gilbert, Judith Plaskow, Robert Fagles, Judith Hemschemeyer, Toi Derricotte, Robert Barton, Susan Kepner, Barry Qualls, Pat Dienstfrey, Betsy Huebner Dubovsky,

Karen Alkalay-Gut, and Martha Smith. My seminar students at Rutgers University have constituted themselves a sacred well of flowing energy, engagement, intelligence, wit, and imagination; their interpretations have continually enriched my own.

Judith Plaskow's workshop on Judaism and Feminism at the 1991 annual Havurah Institute, and Lori Lefkowitz and Leonard Gordon's workshop on Heresy, delightfully stretched my understanding of tradition. The participants in the Genesis Seminar held at the Jewish Theological Seminary—talmudists without a license—show by lively and controversial discussion how endlessly multiple Biblical meanings can be. Audiences at readings and talks have kept me aware of the passion that the Bible inspires, and broadened its meaning for me; I am particularly grateful to the intellectual community at Bucknell University, to Harold Schweizer, who invited me to give the Bucknell Lectures in 1990, and to Catherine Pastore Blair. My rabbi, Susan Schnur, by demonstrating in her life and art the connections among true spirituality, comedy, courage, and the ancient Jewish virtue of lovingkindness—*chesed*—has helped me more than she will ever know. My mother, Beatrice Smith, has been the family archivist—keeper of memories and teacher of values. Kenneth Arnold, my editor at Rutgers, raised at the eleventh hour a set of questions which precipitated a surge of rethinking. Judith Martin Waterman became collaborator as well as copy editor. My husband, Jeremiah Ostriker, continues to be my most invigorating intellectual companion as well as the loving friend who sustains me through periods of confusion and discouragement and holds me to the highest standards of prose writing. To the Research Council of Rutgers University I owe thanks for time in which to meditate and write *ad libitum*; to Kresge College of the University of California-Santa Cruz I owe a beautiful location in which to revise. A grant from the

New Jersey Arts Council in 1992–93 also provided financial support.

I intend *The Nakedness of the Fathers* to speak across Jewish/Christian boundaries, across male/female boundaries, and across the boundaries that separate past from present, daily life from eternity, and the life of the body from that of the spirit. Whether it can or not, is for my readers to decide. I hope, too, that this book will send readers back to the infinitely rich Biblical texts, and inspire them to discover their own meanings there.

Entering the Tents

In the Beginning the Being

*In the beginning God created
the heavens and the earth*
GENESIS 1:1

*The universe expands and contracts
like a great heart.*
ROBINSON JEFFERS

In the beginning the Being
Created heaven and earth
The Being
Created light
The Being
Divided the light   from the darkness
it was evening and morning
The first day.
The Being
Created the firmament
To divide the waters   from the waters
The second day.
The Being
Created grass   herb yielding seed
And fruit tree yielding fruit   whose seed
Is inside of itself

The third day.
The Being
Created lights   in the firmament
Created the sun   and moon
And   made the stars also, the
Fourth day.
The Being
Created great whales
Created sea creatures   winged creatures
And   told them to multiply
The fifth day.
The Being
Told the earth   to bring forth
Animals, and so it gave birth
To all beasts and creeping creatures
The sixth day.
Each day the Being saw   what was made
That it was good   was very good
The Being created the world   without
Language   without pronoun   then
The Being created man and woman
In the image
The distant image
Of itself
And blessed them.

Entering the Tents

Would to God that all the Lord's
people were prophets!
NUMBERS 11:29

You don't want me to dance, too bad,
I'll dance anyhow.
ELIE WIESEL, *THE GATES OF THE FOREST*

I am and am not a Jew. I am a Jew in the sense that every
drop of blood in my veins is Jewish, or so I figuratively
presume although Jews have been a mixed multitude since
they left Egypt. I am a Jew because my parents are. So, naturally, is every thought in my head, my habits of thinking, my
moral impulses and burden of chronic guilt, my sense of
humor if any, my confrontational and adversarial inclina-
tions. They say a Jew is somebody who loves to argue, especially
with God and other Jews. My laughter and tears are Jewish
laughter and tears. What else could they be? My ancestors are
Russian-Jewish ancestors. The shtetl mud is hardly shaken
from my roots. In the 1880's when the great pogroms swept
Russia and eastern Europe, it was me they hated and wanted
to kill. Me, an innocent girl in my babushka throwing grain
to the chickens. In 1944 it could have been me trembling, my
long nose no longer in a book, wetting myself in a railroad
car a few kilometers out of Budapest, or among the soft
stacked bodies like speechless tongues in the mouth of a ravine

5

at Babi Yar. Here is my violin, hidden in a closet of the Warsaw apartment, kicked to splinters by a soldier's boot, going up in flames. And I have fantastically escaped and can breathe air, enjoy freedom, by merest chance. No way I can be anything else. Can't be a Buddhist like Allen Ginsberg (who anyway gets more and more rabbinical), or a Sufi like Doris Lessing. It would be a joke, silly to pretend. When I stand before a classroom to discuss a Shakespeare sonnet, who stands inside me? Isn't it a long row of rabbis waving their bony index fingers, cantankerous and didactic, analyzing a bit of Aramaic phrasing? When I march in a peace demonstration, the prophet Isaiah goes in front of me. Beat your swords into ploughshares, he shouts. Do not hurt or destroy. And I hurry to step and chant alongside him. Could I despise the drops of blood in my body? To deny my Judaism would be like denying the gift of life, the reality of sorrow, the pleasures of learning and teaching. To reject Judaism would be to surrender an idea of justice inseparable from compassion.

But I'm not a Jew, I can't be a Jew, because Judaism repels me as a woman.

To the rest of the world the Jew is marginal. But to Judaism I am marginal. Am woman, unclean. Am Eve. Or worse, am Lilith. Am illiterate. Not mine the arguments of Talmud, not mine the centuries of ecstatic study, the questions and answers twining minutely like vines around the living Word, not mine the Kaballah, the letters of the Hebrew alphabet dancing as if they were attributes of God. These texts, like the Law and the Prophets, are not-me. For a thousand years and longer I am not permitted to discuss sacred writings. I am not permitted to be a scholar. I am not given access to the texts, although my very bones command me to go and study. It is said: Woe to the

*father whose children are girls. It is said: Whoever teaches his
daughter Torah, teaches her obscenity. It is said: The voice of
woman leads to lewdness.*[†] *I am told to light candles in honor
of the holy word, revere my husband and raise my children,
cook and clean and manage a joyous household in the name of
these texts. What right have I to comment? None, none, none.
What calls me to do it? I have no answer but the drops of my
blood, that say* try.

Is there a right of love and anger?

I'm afraid: but it seems obvious, doesn't it. Everyone is
afraid. Do what you fear. *I don't know if it says that in some
text, but women have to run on these hobbled legs, have to
pray and sing with our throttled voices. We have to do it sometime. We have to enter the tents/ texts, invade the sanctuary,*

[†] In traditional Judaism women could not (and among the Orthodox still
cannot) be counted in a minyan or lead religious services; could pray in
synagogue only behind the mechitza, a curtain which separated them from
the males; their testimony (like that of minors, deaf-mutes, and idiots) was
inadmissable in a Jewish court. Whether or not women should study Torah
was debated for centuries, but the dominant view in Talmudic and rabbinic
tradition is that women are endowed with a simple spirituality which should
be centered in the fulfillment of household tasks, the basic moral education
of their children, and the support of their husbands; they should not be
educated as scholars, although the ideal Jew spends his life studying sacred
texts. The most famous exception to the rule that excludes women from
learning is Beruriah, wife of the great rabbi Meir, who became a scholar in
her own right and whose opinions are quoted in Talmud. Legend relates that
Rabbi Meir in order to prove that women were immoral ordered one of his
students to seduce her. After protracted resistance, Beruriah succumbed,
and then killed herself. The rabbinical consensus is that Rabbi Meir's case
was proved, and that learning endangers woman's virtue regardless of her
intelligence.

uncover the father's nakedness. We have to do it, believe it or not, because we love him. It won't kill him. He won't kill us.

Touch me not, thou shalt not touch, command the texts. Thou shalt not uncover. But I shall. Thou shalt not eat it lest ye die. I shall not surely die.

The stories call me simultaneously from outside and from within myself. They are composed, we are told, by a male God dictating them to a male visionary, Moses, so they are composed by not-me. The heroes of the stories are not-me. Likewise the innumerable generations of commentators, who until now have been not-me, but wise and learned men who would consider it improper or perhaps sacrilegious for a woman to express opinions regarding Scripture. What then compels me to comment? What made me recognize when I first read these tales that I had known them always, as if they were dreams of my own that I had forgotten? The tales of the tribe. My tribe, therefore my stories. The shapes my soul has always unconsciously or half-consciously assumed. But to say this is to say nothing. What do the stories mean to me and what do I mean to them? I cannot tell until I write.

(To make each story open to me, as I climb into and into it. To make each story open, as I climb down into its throat.)

&#xFFFD;

Who reads here? Who writes here? A mixed multitude. It is not merely woman distinct from man. I define myself as a child of exile, diasporic, dispersed. A child moreover of the Enlightenment, squeezed from knowledge's apple. Pressed like juice from the pulp of secular science, art, literature, philosophy. After halakhah comes haskalah.[†] Two centuries distilled, a swallow of that hard cider. My cosmos has been expanding for approximately fifteen billion years. My galaxy is one among numberless hurtling systems, my sun is an average star which will someday burn out, my speck of a planet is composed of stone two-thirds covered by water, and my species is a species of mammal. Do not ask me to worship a tribal diety instead of the universal Creator. Do not expect me to forget, either, that the people of the Book are my people, and their God my God. And do not think I am unaware of this contradiction.

My case is (something like) that of the poet Emily Dickinson, who worshiped and did not worship the Father, or the poet H.D. who worshiped Isis and Aphrodite along with Jesus, or the poet Anne Sexton who asked Is it true? Is it true? and imagined that she was Christ and imagined that she was Mary, and believed that God eats beautiful women. My case is (something like) that of the poet William Blake who declared "Everything that lives is holy" and "All deities reside in the human breast." But it is also like that of Franz Kafka: "What do I have in common with Jews? I have hardly anything in common with myself."

[†] Halakhah (rabbinic law; metaphorically "way," as it shares a root with the verb to walk) has come to represent "normative" traditional Judaism. Haskalah (enlightenment) was an intellectual social movement within Judaism which spread from Berlin throughout eastern Europe from the mid-eighteenth century to the end of the nineteenth. Its goals included modernization of Jewish life, development of Jewish culture and literature, and participation of Jews in European humanist culture. It proposed that one might be a Jew and yet a citizen of the world. The education of women was one of its priorities.

Or Baruch Spinoza, lens grinder of tolerant Amsterdam, into whose focus the divinity of Nature enters. Or those later heretics Marx, Trotsky, Rosa Luxemburg, Emma Goldman, believers in political transformation and the historical imperative. Revolutionaries struggling to combine the fire of justice from Sinai with the light of reason from Europe.

Or it is (something) like that of Solomon, who builds the Temple and cries out on its accomplishment: "Behold, the heaven of heavens cannot contain thee; how much less this house which I have builded." Or that of the rabbis who, brooding over the Word, declare that "there is always another interpretation." Behind every speculation the yearning of King David, whose soul pants after God as the hart pants after the water brook. Or the call of the Shulamite who rises, and goes about the city in the streets, and in the broad ways seeks him whom her soul loveth. Reader, my case is like yours, perhaps. Whether you call yourself Jew, Christian, Pagan, Atheist, Goddess-worshipper, who cares what you call yourself. Perhaps your case is like mine. A case of (some kind of) love.

🈂

When I am small my mother and father walk around the Brooklyn apartment naked because it is so hot, it is summer. I am naked too, I sit on the sticky linoleum in front of the electric fan. We listen to the war news on the radio, we listen to Jack Benny, my father does a little dance, dingle dangle, he is so funny.

I wake in the dark, listening to the steam pipes knock in the new apartment. Outside my window tea-colored snow is milling coldly under the streetlamp. My bed feels cold under me, then I realize it is wet. I pull the chenille spread from my bed, wrap it around myself for a cloak, tiptoe through the darkness to my parents' room, and push open their door. What strikes my senses first is an odor new to me: pungent, briny, and sweet. In an instant my eyes can already make out my mother and father moving under their blanket, hugging tightly, and something in my head is already shouting Mine! Mine!

We are walking along the East River Drive, hand in hand. My mother is in a good mood, she's singing. We are going to Thomas Jefferson Park where we grow vegetables in the victory garden, it is April and we will rake the ground, later the corn will be far over my head with red and purple petunias along the borders. I take the opportunity to ask something I was wondering about. Can I marry daddy when I grow up. She does not hesitate but answers immediately that if I still want to when I grow up, I can. By this I understand that I cannot. I understand further that she is not angry. I see that I have asked a question of profound weight and have been answered with profound, quick-witted love.

He takes me to Coney Island by subway. I go on the amusement park rides while he watches, because we can't afford for both of us to do it. He leans on the railing wearing a light tan cotton jacket, waving to me whenever I come around. We have tuna fish sandwiches and oranges in a paper bag, the oranges leave my fingers sticky. Then we wait on the boardwalk for the fireworks. When it is dark they let off the fireworks, we listen to the booming, we watch sprays and cascades of color illuminate the sky, we say oh, oh, along with the crowd, until they make an American flag out of colored lights over the ocean water. That is the finale. Afterward we travel home by subway, an hour and a half, first the El then the tunnel, I fall asleep on his shoulder, then we walk the three blocks home in the summer dark through city fragrances.

My father is a Union man. He comes home from the meeting, my mother and I are waiting up. "There once was a Union maid, Who never was afraid," he sings lustily. "She went to the Union hall, When a meeting there was called, And when the company boys came round, She always stood her ground." My mother and I join in the chorus. "Oh you can't scare me, I'm sticking to the Union." He believes in the brotherhood of mankind, so does my mother, we all do; it is my impression that everyone does.

My mother reads Robert Burns, "A man's a man for a' that." She reads Edna St. Vincent Millay, "God, I can push the grass apart, And lay my finger on Thy heart." She recites "Give me your tired, your poor, your huddled masses yearning to breathe free." She reads me Shakespeare, Browning, and dozens of other poets. Sometimes she will not speak to my father for a day or a week. Or else she shouts at him. He is a quiet shy man like all the men in my family, and when she shouts he disappears into silence.

He never hits me. He never gives me orders or disciplines me; that is her job, which she performs by making long rational speeches about the issues. But he has some wishes. He doesn't want me to go away to college. He wants me to stay in the city, go to City College or Hunter College, marry a nice boy. A Jewish boy he means although he does not say so. But this is not his decision, she is on my side, I am going to leave. I do leave. We quarrel for the first time on my first visit home when he makes fun of "modern art." It turns out he does not like Kafka either. I quarrel with him over Kafka, I am furious and superior. Probably I am angry because when I walked through the door of the apartment, and they stood up from their armchairs in the living room, I saw that my mother and father were old.

The stories are part of a book compiled over a span of perhaps a thousand years, equivalent to the time between Beowulf and T.S. Eliot, and edited for a period lasting from about four hundred years before the birth of Jesus to over a hundred years afterward. A thick quilt, patchwork, braiding, embroidery. No single author. Multiple authors. Some threads of language go back to Phoenician, Hittite, Ugaritic, Sumerian poems. The stories form a sequence which is itself a story, the tale of our, that is my, long relationship with God.

Reader, you are supposed to ask: does God exist. Is the Holy One in that book real or imagined. And then what about Abraham, Moses, and so on, what is their status vis-à-vis "reality." Is Abraham in other words a body, a material fact, or is he a spirit, an imagined fact. I confess these questions do not interest me. For who among us, solid flesh though we are, is not partially fictional. And who among us supposes herself the inventor of her own fiction. And who is not just such an aggregation of scraps, just such a patchwork as Abraham, a basket containing millennia. Is God a myth? A set of myths? Then so am I, so are you.

Let me suppose that Abraham is an imagined fact. Let me suppose that God is another. Let me suppose that I am a third. We are all equally real in the dimension of language, which is where we intersect. It is here that we meet, marry, wrestle, bargain, love and fear one another, find ecstasy and desolation, form some kind of tangled ganglia, push and pull one another forward in the story.

The story of history, the movement into and through time. In the beginning, in Genesis, there is much more woman. As in myths, as in dreams, or as in families. In one telling of the story it is said that woman and man are alike, at the very beginning, created simultaneously in the image of their creator. In another it is said that woman is more powerful, more intellectual, more ambitious and daring than her mate, he a first draft made of mud, she the improved version.[†] Then man gradually becomes more powerful, while woman continues to act, laugh, talk, and in part control the course of the narrative. Later there is less and less woman. As in most nation states. As in "public" life. As in law, theology, and war. After the Exodus women start to become insignificant. Shepherds and their domestic stories be-

---

[†] The two creation narratives in Genesis provide the most familiar example of the redactors' attempts to join accounts from heterogeneous sources. In Genesis 1–1:3 the simultaneous creation of male and female earthlings climaxes the creation of nature and is followed by the sabbath; but in Genesis 1:4–3:19 God creates first man, then other animals, then woman, and the woman proceeds to show all the initiative in the story. These and similar textual inconsistencies ("fault lines" to Geoffrey Hartman, "the abrasive frictions, the breaks, the discontinuities of readability" to Roland Barthes) make Scripture a garden of delight to the exegete, the theologian, the mystic, and the poet such as myself. I return again and again to these places of mystery.

come warriors and their military stories. The penis, that flexible flesh, hardens into the metal of the sword.

> The sword thins to the sceptre.
> The sceptre dictates and the pen is born.

Myth moves forward into legend, legend melts into history. Annals, records, myths, legends, rituals, laws converge: they become the accepted canon, the official texts. The women disappear, they cease to act, they become objects of the law, they become property, they become unclean, they become a snare, they become a metaphor. The disappearance of the women is the condition and consequence of the male covenant. Meanwhile at every step the men advance into individuality. No two alike. Forward march our patriarchs, our heroes, our judges, our kings. Abraham, Isaac, Jacob, Joseph. Moses and Joshua. Samuel, Saul, David, Solomon. They carry populations in their loins, in their orbits, in their mysterious magnetic fields. They embody and enact the will of the Holy One, enduring the lava of punishments and promises poured over their covenanted heads. Their circumcision the sign of the covenant.

My fathers, whom I intend to pursue. Their stories mine. My fathers, whose meanings I am laboring to understand, since to understand them is to understand myself. Needing to know whom I love, whom I hate. Needing to remember that I am my fathers, just as much as I am my mothers.

Yet the beginning is not the beginning. Inside the oldest stories are older stories, not destroyed but hidden. Swallowed. Mouth songs. Wafers of parchment, layer underneath layer. Nobody knows how many. The texts retain traces, leakages, lacunae, curious figures of speech, jagged irruptions. What if I say these traces too are mine? If I pull at the texts like the yard worker who goes out with a rake in early spring. She pulls at the compacted layers of leaves, heaving them up from the ground. Wet and soggy, they resist, they cling to the earth. She stands in the yard sniffing the fresh air. Under the compost there is bare ground from which a few thin chartreuse sprouts have begun to uncurl. A dog barks somewhere in the neighborhood. Another beginning, I tell myself. Nor is the canonized text a final text, nor can the writing be finished. For I remember slavery; I remember liberation from slavery. This is what the Lord did for me when I came out of Egypt. I remember a covenant in which I promised to serve God's purposes. And what if I say the purposes have not yet been all revealed?

> They say no, they say blasphemer, they say false,
> They say whore, they say bitch, they say witch,
> They say ignorant woman, they lock me up for crazy

Of course I'm crazy
Digging and digging
Smelling the ground
I talk to myself and see things
I remember things, and sometimes I remember
My time when I was powerful, bringing birth
My time when I was just, composing law
My time playing before the throne
When my name was woman of valor
When my name was wisdom
And what if I say the Torah is
My well of living waters
Mine

❧ *As in Myth* ❧

The Garden

The Garden

And God said, Let us make man in our image,
after our likeness. . . . So God created man in his
own image, in the image of God created he him;
male and female created he them.
GENESIS 1:26–27

. . . Flowers of all hue, and without thorn the rose.
JOHN MILTON

*B*etween a child and a parent there is a game that is special, the first game we play, the game-of-games, compared with which no game in later life attains equal intensity because none is equally pure. In its most pure form this is a game without props and tools. This is not a contest. This is a game about identity and power, it is a game about playing.[†]

[†] I offer this story or this game, *al que quiere*, about the origins of personal identity, as an alternative to the versions of Freud and other psychoanalytic theorists, and as a personal variation upon the theme of the garden which begins in Genesis and proliferates throughout western writing. If it appears here that the figures of God, Mother, and Lover are mingled, and perhaps even identified with the garden that is their setting, and if, besides, in the dialectic of Presence and Absence which is the foundation of all love and therefore of all identity I have made Presence the primary experience, it is because I believe an important truth about the origins of spirituality has been forgotten and needs to be remembered. For the same reason, and in a conscious inversion of the biblical narrative sequence, I place my reading of the Garden, into and from which we were all born, prior to Creation.

It is a game about myself. I absolutely exist and yet I might not exist, my existence might be contingent. It is the game the first game about reality, the truth, and therefore about lies, the false, and therefore about the former's need for the latter—what is a truth without a lie? To create the truth. What is the first truth I can hide? My own existence. By hiding I become certain of it. By hiding I become (certain of it).

Between a child and a parent the initial game is hiding and showing. At first the parent takes the initiative, leading the child into the game. The child is lying flat on her back in the crib, kicking her heels rhythmically, gazing devotedly up at the face of the parent, who gazes in the usual devoted way down at her. Now the parent has the impulse to stimulate extra happiness. So she covers her face with her hands for two seconds, then removes her hands, beaming at the child, who instantly breaks into chuckles, wriggling her fat body and beating her fists and feet against the crib mattress. Every time the parent plays I'm-gone-I'm-here, the child laughs, gurgles. To laugh is to understand. To understand is to laugh. Later the child herself will play I'm-gone-I'm-here, putting her fat hands over her face, perhaps peeking through the fingers but confident that she herself is invisible or rather pretending to be invisible and then opening her hands or flinging them apart to show her radiant face. Everyone agrees how much this is fun and funny. There is toothless smiling and laughing, there is shrieking with glee. Later the child learns that others are willing to play the same game. I am. You are. We like babies.

We are all mammals together having fun. By now the interpretations are already so multifoliate, the baby's "I" so confident, thanks to its discreet tolerance of insecurity, so powerfully aware that it is loved, so confirmed in its presence by its imaginary absence, and so identical to and different from this one and that one among its lovers who come and go. It sees that it is an idol. It sees what adoration is where earlier it only adored the other and now it imitates and adores itself. Later it hides in the closet behind the overcoats to frighten the parents, then jumps out to frighten them and make them happy and show power.

Only before this game is played the child doesn't exist. Or rather the child wholly exists, is even wholly aware of existing, yet is aware of nothing. When the child comes into the world, out of the mother's hole, and they catch it in the square cotton cloth and lift it up, a gift, everything is present. The baby is wholly there, naked, damp, red, wrinkled, coming. The eyes are the most intelligent of any mammal, they stare through the cold three dimensional world, and things start increasing and multiplying fast, *I'm here, here, here,* what cannot the child do, what force cannot it exercise, yet it isn't there at all, nothing is there.

Just the same, when Adam comes out of God's hole, he is perfect as a doll. He can walk run leap, he can climb, he learns to swim with no trouble, he can feed himself, he can talk think speculate, he names every animal correctly by its true name that the Divine Being has already given, which comes intuitively to his lips, he can only not fly because the angels and demons were jealous. He's all there, burning like a fire, flowing like water, transparent as air. A perfect whole. The same with Eve, the rib-marrow, the dancing feet, the crisp hairs, the mind as fleet as a bird. Another perfect whole or rather part of the identical one. God places the couple inside this garden, carefully so as not to knock things over, and enjoys watching them play—as it were inside the crib bars—smiling an indulgent parental smile. When they make love, kissing sucking biting licking rolling over, caressing pinching scratching, entering and removing, ecstatically blending and dividing, God gazes at them devotedly and sometimes adds a bouquet of flowers, strewing the blossoms around them in a careless circle, or shows them a patch of moss, or perches a nightingale on a branch just beyond view, for them to listen to.

Something is still missing. For their brains, those ripening walnuts, are as wide as the sky but also as blank as clouds. Forming, flowing, diffuse, changing and lovely, their minds retain no shape, have need of none. No need of an identity, or a memory, they to whom the world is an omnipresent nipple.

Then the Divine One decides to play the game with them. Instead of being always there whenever they look, wherever they look, the Divine One withdraws for a few moments just while they are in the midst of looking, telling or showing something—then returns. Startled at first by the oddity of an environment lacking God, starting to sniff for the God-smell and listen perplexedly for the God-music, they soon learn that the game is a game, and can play it themselves.

❧

My beloved is mine and I am hers
We are feeding among the lilies

🖾

As Torah existed two thousand years before the creation of heaven and earth, written with black fire on white fire, and lay in God's lap intoning the world's history in ladderlike cantillations, so I too am writing, am music, am sculpted according to design, am drawn by a pattern that both precedes and succeeds me. And as the twenty-two letters descending from God's crown already knew the words they were to form, so I know myself mother of all living, my ovaries burdened and abundant at my birth. I can hear the chirping of the eggs.

The beloved being a gateway into my garden which opens into another garden, I perceive God lightly and sweetly tumbling within him as an embryo within its sac. Around his neck is a chain of jasmine.

Some parts of the pleasure: his likeness to me, his intelligence, his math and physics, his eye mischievously spangling, his shoulders shrugging, his reticence, the tender flesh along his sides, his strength, the translucent milk in his breasts, his strangeness, his timid bud.

🖾

ADAM: She is "taken out" of me: is made of my interior, my inward lines of thought, to be a mirror to me, as the silk lining of a coat is used for a dress: so she "takes and eats" the fruit as she was "taken:" oh my lady, snaky Eve

Deceived and forgotten, the better to bite
To undo fiber, untwist a rope, dissolve, disintegrate

One flesh
The better to bait it
One poison for us both

EVE: He forgets that the garden was my garden. My tree, my spiral snakes, my attributes, my happiness was that I was, oh leaf. My knowledge, my power, what a yielding fruit. And he forgets that I made him: mud mother.

ADAM: Never, never to fly above earth or to go far underneath it. This was wrongly done. Also water, we can't breathe in it, I'm angry. (He swings a stick, soft grey crenelated material comes out, along with blood. What he can chew he eats. He knocks bananas down that can't be reached, this is a stick, and he joyously eats the bananas. Now he is tired. He bangs with a stick on the hard ground. Dear mother, let me in.)

EVE: Listen, talk to me, let me explain. (She cannot believe he has forgotten the dialogues with the animals. He denies everything, he claims he never understood their languages. Maybe *you* did, *you're* the natural one, he grumbles. It makes her almost cry with exasperation. Remember, she wants to say, how witty the birds were? How timid the earthworms? Remember how the horses would lose their patience and interrupt? But if she reminds him, he hits her.)

🏵

I'm sitting in the sandbox early in the morning. I have all day. I pat the dimpled sand, feel it rubbing under my legs, getting in my socks and underpants. To make sand-pies you dig in the wet part underneath. You pack it in your sand pail, not too hard, then fast turn the sand pail over, press it into the sand, then tap the top then pull the pail off careful-ly. Sometimes they crumble right away. If perfect, a section of a slightly tapered cylinder, you can stick an ice cream stick in the top.

My place where I am working is nice. I have six finished sand pies lined up. The square concrete frame of the sandbox is far away from where I am, I'm in the middle. My mother sits on a wooden bench watching me with a magazine in her lap. Behind the bench is a sycamore tree which I often look up at. Very far off, surrounding me, there are swings, a slide, seesaws, monkey bars, concrete water fountain, more trees, chain link playground fence, and beyond that are the brick houses with the sun on them, and past them a few blocks away are some stores where we always go shopping. In the other direction is the subway entrance.

If another child comes, my happiness is fractured. If I were Eve and God my mother, I would be happier without Adam.

Later however I'm with my boyfriend under the bridge. Hand in hand we go off and get into some woods, where we kiss in the shade until I think I'll die with rapture. This is it. It's what I was born for. I reach my arms around his flannel shirt. Smell the mulchy leaves. My fingers feel the meat of his back, my body rests against his chest, peaceful, protected, transmitting a power. His face seems an angel's to me, it is almost too beautiful. I know mine seems the same to him, creates the same ecstasy and nimbus of apprehension. We learned this love in the movies and on the radio. But we were prepared to learn it. Ready to learn like newborn sparrows learning their parental song—it was ours already. Our inheritance, into which we grew. The beams of sex batter us, butter us, better us. We're growing now, we're multiplying right and left like tomatoes.

Yet we never talk about it. Why not? Words unnecessary during the touching, inadequate afterward, and others would sneer leer jeer make us ashamed.

> *The first is the first, forever*
> *and forever lost. I try*
> *to remember.*

The labia of the fountain slap. We hide and sleep. High in the air streams spray, and cascade down. Circulating between their subterranean pipes and the air of the park, the streams of water seem fictional, ethereal, like the cycles of economics. Imaginary things we agree to treat as real. Along the paths of the park are stone statues of naked men and women. Lawns, lanes, shrubbery, cusps of granite outcrop, iron spiked fences. Large yellow leaves littering the gravel.

Don't let the fountain stop. Now you, now we, have drowned

ourselves in odors. They call to us from the turnstile at the entrance. *Aren't you coming back?* We cup our hands. *No, we cry.* Our voices are swallowed in the crowd's rush. There is a torrent of exiting citizens. Laborers, delinquent boys on skateboards, sheeplike ancient shufflers, shouting students eating their final snacks, dogs on leashes, homosexual couples, pairs of adolescent boyfriends and girlfriends holding nail-bitten hands but, through embarrassment, not looking at each other. Tired families with small children close to tears. What was an entrance path in the morning, along which visitors strolled in a leisurely spacious way, is now the path of egress; for the gates are about to close.

Now it is night. The guards have circled the paths, searching for strays. The moon has cleared the trees, like a single headlight.

Awhile ago three boys from the neighborhood jumped the fence of the grizzlies, and swam the moat around their granite island. The moon was full that night too, and gilded the trees and cement, but what they had in mind is impossible to guess. Did they hope merely to see the grizzlies up close, to feed them, to tease them with sticks and stones? Did they taste the addictive joy of disobedience? Perhaps it was a sacrifice. Two of the boys escaped, leaving their clothing stacked on a rock. The third was partially devoured.

🖾

The reader breathes . . .
Reader you may breathe a sigh of relief. Reader you may thank God for death, without which there's no story. Reader imagine

yourself imprisoned in paradise dying of wholesomeness dying of health dying for a grain of poison.

Innanna spreads the bridal sheet, she welcomes her shepherd husband. She tells the people: Dumuzi lays hands on my holy vulva, he smooths my black boat with cream, he quickens my narrow boat with milk. I caress his loins and decree a sweet fate for him.

Krishna leans over Radha, her breasts as ripe as melons to his hands. He says that her breath carries the odor of all flowering plants as if it were incense drifting toward heaven. She blushes and lowers her head. The servants depart.

The king has brought the Shulamite into his house. She is black and comely, she kisses him with the kisses of her mouth, comparing him to an apple tree among the trees of the wood. She says: let him come into the garden and eat the pleasant fruits.

Creation

So many versions, so many visions, each one sacred, here is one. God was originally a female who gave birth to a male companion. He refused to live in a state of equality with her, and so he ate her. Swallowed her whole.[†] Regretting this act

---

[†] Does anyone any longer doubt the priority of the Great Goddess? Statues of Near Eastern goddesses can be dated from 25,000 B.C.E., millennia prior to any male gods. In Near Eastern myth, as Raphael Patai observes, "the earliest answers to the great question of 'Whence?' all reiterate, in various forms, the same idea: it was out of the body of the primordial goddess that the world-egg emerged or that the earth was born; or alternately, it was the goddess' body itself that provided the material from which the earth was made." And the eating of her? Gerda Lerner summarizes: "The observable pattern is: first, the demotion of the Mother-Goddess figure and the ascendance and later dominance of her male consort/son; then his merging with a storm-god into a male Creator-God, who heads the pantheon of gods and goddesses. Wherever such changes occur, the power of creation and of fertility is transferred from the Goddess to the God."

when it was too late, he created the universe. First he produced electromagnetic field equations, then subatomic particles to oscillate between nonexistence and existence, and finally galaxies with their stars and planets like milk clots. Later he made Adam and Eve, the earthling followed by his wife or life,[†] hoping that they would become his companions, much as a man begins to write a novel to console himself for a particular loss and knows it is a good novel when the characters start behaving independently. He needed someone to talk to, someone to talk to him, some peculiar combination of order and disorder. The crucial creative decision was inventing a prohibition for the man and his wife, which they would inevitably violate, and from which the interesting action would follow.

Here is another. God is originally a compound being, simultaneously male and female.[‡] They create the world cooperatively. They create the animals in two genders and when they decide

---

[†] The name Adam derives from ha-adam, the earth, from which he is formed. Chava, Eve, derives from chai, life; cf. her title "Mother of all living," a title also held by a variety of goddesses; that the name is also related to the tetragrammaton, YHWH, suggests that the Hebrew God may at some point have been conceived of as a sacred pair.

[‡] An androgynous creator is suggested by the Hebrew term elohim, plural in form, signifying divine being(s). Elohim is always translated "God" in English, and scholars typically insist that it is not (and presumably never was) a true plural. Why not? When referring to pagan gods it is understood to be plural. When referring to the Hebrew god it usually takes singular verbs and adjectives, but not always; cf. elohim hayyim, always translated "the living God," but literally "the living Gods." The term elohim appears upward of 2,000 times in the Hebrew Bible, most startlingly in Genesis 1:26–27, translated by the King James Version: "And God (elohim) said, let us make man in our image, after our likeness. . . . Male and female created he them." If not an actual plural, the term would be the equivalent of a collective

to create Adam and Eve in their own image naturally they give
them two genders also, for the sake of maximal fourfold pleasure, mixing and mingling. Quarreling unfortunately ensues as
in any commune. In this case the males bond together, God
with Man; as do the females, Goddess with Woman; each pair
sulks and devises incriminating stories about the selfishness of
the other pair. The females accuse the males of being aggres-
sive. The males accuse the females of being hysterical. They
drink the cup of bitterness. They surrender to the temptation of
sorrow.

At first the One. Then dividing and dividing. Light from darkness. The waters above from the waters below. Day from night.
Female from male. Splittings.

🕸

Not I, not I, but the wind that blows through me. Wind,
spirit, the breath, ruach (fem. Hebrew), spiritus (masc.
Latin). A mother on the face of the waters. A father.
Create. Said of the divine agent: To bring into being, cause to
exist; to produce where nothing was before, "to form out of
nothing." *Like truth from lies.* Creation. The action or process
of creating. The fact of being so created. The action of making.
"This bodiless creation exstasie/ Is very cunning in." "In our
fine arts, not imitation, but creation, is the aim." That which
God has created; the created world; creatures collectively. An
original production of human intelligence or power, especially of

---

singular. Is it the ubiquity of this term that causes the vision of an androgynous Godhead in the Zohar? Phyllis Trible's account of the implied male-
female God in Genesis concentrates on this passage.

the imagination. *What it comes to in any case is that I make words sentences poems paragraphs books, without knowing either why I do so, where they appear from, or where having taken form they disperse themselves. If it is correct to say I imagine them, who or what then is the "I" in question, who is she, she who is I.*

▩

In a third version God transcends gender, is not even a person, creates the universe and man and woman by accident, and gradually over the aeons becomes absent from them while emitting a long withdrawing roar.

So many versions, so many visions. The only improbable story is that God was originally male.

▩

A crowd of children in new school clothing and soap smell was in the room ahead of me. There is so much talking shouting whispering I can't follow, colored poster paper flowers butterflies on classroom windows, dust motes, high ceilings. The endless grey smeared wall on which I am trying to make the first letter of my name the new way: a*. Over and over the chalk creates* e*. Wrong wrong wrong. Shame confusion anger. The children stare, my teacher frowns. After eternity, triumph and mastery.* a a a*, and back to desk trembling.*

Clean smooth paper emanates potency. Mine, mine! The good smell. The deep. The unwritten. The undrawn. Stacked untouched rectangles, notebooks swept by emptiness, sign of infinity.

Yellow bevelled wooden cylinder, Mother says stop chewing my pencil—

I lean so hard on the crayon that it breaks.

The Brothers

*And the Lord had respect unto Abel and his
offering. But unto Cain and his offering he had
not respect. And Cain was very wroth, and his
countenance fell. . . and it came to pass, when they
were in the field, that Cain rose up against Abel
his brother, and slew him.*

GENESIS 4:4–8

*Cain is amazed. His big hand gropes
inside the butchered throat before him:
from where does the silence burst?*

DAN PAGIS

*D*ividing proliferates, proliferation divides, whether we
like it or not, in order to get from the One to the Many.
Light divides from darkness, the waters divide from the waters,
man divides from woman, brother from brother. And just as
Eden contracts like a womb to expel Adam and Eve, so the
advent of siblings ensures inequality which creates psychic pain
which precipitates aggression: to make a long story short, awful
as it is, at some (early) point we have to have the first murder.
We have to.

Blood soaks the ground. Nobody says it is very good, or even
very logical: the animal offered as sacrifice, and the grain

offered as an offering, had no idea they were in competition. God too is confused. He doesn't know exactly why he wanted to choose between the two, preferring one. He only knows that he had to.

⬛

I loved being born
I hated it

I loved being your brother
I hated you

They were beautiful parents
They liked you better

I hated being beaten in the head
What excitement

I hated dying
You deserved it

My blood cries from the ground
Shut up, shut up

⬛

While the blood of Abel cries from the ground, God allies himself with Cain. What choice does he have now? He too is responsible for death. He too is glad to be alive, bursting with life, unwilling to die. He too is ready to be a nomad. He marks the forehead of the shivering Cain so that nobody will kill him. Then he takes his wrist. Mark me, God says to Cain, here in the middle of my furrowed forehead, with that mixture of ashes and mud on your finger. And now move.

Survival

*And it came to pass . . . that the waters of the flood
were upon the earth. . . . And every living
substance was destroyed.*
GENESIS 7:10

*Are you ashamed because you are alive in the place
of another?. . . You cannot block out such feelings.*
PRIMO LEVI, *THE DROWNED AND THE SAVED*

They did what they were told. The animals two by two, like toys, made the children giggle. When the rain started, pocks on a dry ground causing it to steam up, they were ready. They went inside and listened. The neighbors had never had a clue. The rain came down harder. Noah and his family were alone in that semi-darkness with the pairs of living creatures. They sat close and listened to the roaring storm. After many days, they felt their boat lift and begin to rock.

Then it was as if time stopped. Rain fell, wind blew, waves knocked against the hull. Mostly he and his family were sick. Crawling over the mounds of animal and human bodies, they felt boneless as worms and stank as much as the other beasts. Their noises became indistinguishable from bleats roars whinnyings. Noah put his head out a window only once, hoping to breathe cooler air. Rain was hissing. The water was crowded with the swollen dead. Men women children. He saw them in a lightning flash. They flung their arms toward him, like infants to a mother. He gasped, slammed the shutters closed, threw himself to the floor.

Spring, and when the rains stopped the streets would fill with children. We stamped in the puddles, sent twigs floating down the streams in the gutters, went to the park to play with the mud. If the rain had been a long, soaking one, there would be worms wriggling on the sidewalk along the patches of grass. One time I watched some boys have a contest, stepping on worms and keeping score how many they got.

When they caught me looking, I ran away across the splashy street. In a square of wet dirt under a thin tree, two more pink worms lay quietly. Two temptations.

When the boat beached on Ararat and Noah climbed out, it was hard at first to walk on motionless land, he staggered like an invalid, and could hardly bear the shock of daylight and color. To make a clearing he and his sons had to haul away the debris, including rotted tree trunks and the bones of drowned creatures, often with seaweed and flesh dangling together. On the third morning Noah went to the shore where the boat lay vacantly on its side. He walked around it examining his workmanship. The proportions of the ship noble. Good tongue and groove construction. Seams tight. Where the tar was absorbed the wood was silvered, felt like satin to the touch. He examined the barnacles, the clinging encrustation, fierce to be alive. He told his boys to make axes. By nightfall there was a pile of salt-caked wood as tall as a house. By dawn it was black coals, glowering red, resisting death as long as they could.

Noah let the bed of coals die quietly, not interfering. He had all the time in the world. Throughout the night he had watched the fire take its course, thinking how pleasurable it was to destroy the work of his own hands. The heat blast, the furious red crackle hurled upward, tremendously far above his head, the imaginary bodies writhing in the flame and escaping, the slow subsiding. It made him feel, he thought, like God.

Fire against water. Noah opened his shuttered mind to that red energy. It almost erased the countless bloated fingers.

The Father's Nakedness

And he drank of the wine, and was drunken;
and he was uncovered within his tent.
And Ham, the father of Canaan,
saw the nakedness of his father,
and told his two brethren without.
GENESIS 9:21–22

"No!" cried his father, cutting short
the answer, threw the blankets off with
a strength that sent them all flying
in a moment and sprang erect in bed. . . .
"You wanted to cover me up, I know,
my young sprig,
but I'm far from being covered up yet."
FRANZ KAFKA, "THE JUDGMENT"

I thought the vineyard idea was a good one, the old man had to be kept busy somehow. Then he started drinking. Steadily. After all we had been through. The pity of it. And would lie in his tent uncovered, naked and sweating. Father, how could I turn my back. I wanted to cover your pathetic flabby body.

I told my brothers: our father is lying naked in the tent, dead drunk. They said no. That doesn't happen in families like ours. Only gentiles are alcoholics. Shut up, they said, and quickly

turned their backs. Then our father woke up and began screaming, cursing me.

You'll be black, he screamed. The sweat stood out on his forehead. You'll never get anywhere. Your children will be slaves
and servants.[†] He retched and flung himself backward shivering. That ought to teach you respect, he screamed.

[†] Noah's curse (Genesis 9:25) is actually only against Ham's son Canaan,
dooming him to be "the lowest servant" or "slave of slaves" to his brothers.
Scholars speculate that the passage was composed during a period when the
Canaanites were subjected to the Israelites. However, the generalized iden-
tification of "children of Ham" or "sons of Ham" with black Africans was
used by advocates of the slave trade in the modern West, and continues to be
used as a religious rationale by white supremacists.

The Rainbow

And I, behold, I establish my covenant with you,
and with your seed after you.
GENESIS 9:9

The mountain trembles in the dark lake,
its golden cliffs dipping
from almost-sunset light
deep into almost-evening waters.
DENISE LEVERTOV

When the flood receded, the rainbow flew above the Caucasus. Looking down, it saw its reflection in a mountain lake, sparkling amid the serene turquoise depths. Beautiful illusion, it said, I represent the enduring mercy of the Holy One, who, perceiving that the imagination of man's heart is evil from his youth, nonetheless promises never again to curse the ground for his sake. Beautiful illusion, replied the swimming reflection, I represent the enduring mercy of humankind, who, perceiving that the heart of the Holy One loves destruction, nonetheless promises never to curse the cosmos for his sake.

Myth into Legend

The Fathers I

The Bosom of Abraham

*Now the Lord had said unto Abram, Get thee out
of thy country, and from thy kindred, and from thy
father's house, unto a land that I will show thee . . .
and I will bless thee, and make thy name great;
and thou shalt be a blessing.*
GENESIS 12:7

*It is wise to agree that all things are one. The
ordering cosmos the same for all. Everliving fire,
in measures kindled and in measures going out. . . .
Immortals are mortal, mortals immortal, living
the others' death, dying the others' life.*
HERACLITUS

A young man hears a voice: the surrounding hills talking
in unison with the sky. It is in his head. The young man
observes an eagle circling his head, bees around a thistle, dust
streaks across his feet. Everything looks like a design. He knows
what he hears is God's voice, what else could it be. He feels like
a lamb newly led to pasture, one long muscle of pleasure.

*When I think of Abraham I remember my grandfathers,
as if they are the lenses through which I see him. He is
something extraordinary, completely different from
Adam and Noah. Adam is my first father, Noah is a second
Adam, they represent birth and survival, they are fathers of
the species.*

49

Who then is Abraham, not myth but legend, progenitor not of my species but of my tribe. To ask is like unfolding from an envelope a letter announcing that I have won a prize. My shred of meaning stems from this complicated life suddenly emerging from a thicket of simple begettings, its story a combination of scraps coarsely stitched together. A migratory legend, a domestic comedy, a shamanistic vision, a military interpolation, a parable of international diplomacy, a bloody ritual of origin, a piece from here and a piece from there, adding up to the tribal ancestor.

Father Abraham is neither king, general, prophet, or priest, but an obscure shepherd whose newly circumcised loins produce in old age a particular seed, representing a particular idea. A set of promises tied to a set of commands. A chromosomal libretto. A knotted unbroken fiber, twisting and untwisting from one generation to the next. Four thousand years later, much against the odds, as historians have noted, the idea remains alive, alive, alive and propagating. Still reproducing itself.

Today, says Walt Whitman, I am jetting the stuff of far more arrogant republics. And in the distance is Abraham, jetting the stuff of a chosen people. Out of which, like a mist, I twist and arise.

The voice instructs him to leave home, along with his wife, to travel to a place which it will show him. Go, it says. Your seed will be numerous as the dust of the earth. And I will bless you. And to all nations you will be a blessing. The young man

Abram inquires the meaning of blessing. It means that a living being is singled out to become more and more itself, more and more alive. To ferment with aliveness. To grow like bread rising.

A burning country follows: contours of mountains, settlements of dirty stone, palms, pools. The animals lick his hands with their rough tongues. Once he builds a shrine. Sometimes at dawn the voice is like a sparrow guarding its nest. At noon like a carpenter sawing wood. A buzz in the workshop. Sometimes the voice is like thunderclouds unfolding, unfolding, still dry. Always a highway, always hills. Finally it tells him to look in all directions, length and breadth: this land will be given to him and his seed, who will be countless as the stars. Good, he thinks. When the voice informs him that the children will be enslaved for four hundred years in Egypt he feels confused, a horror of great darkness, but the voice promises to carry them forth with a strong hand. He will bear them as on eagles' wings to this land, where they will be his people, and he will be their God. Very good! Abram shouts, delighted at the greenery of the land. The voice becomes his friend, then, it advises him on all his journeys. Also, it confirms that the universe is One, which Abram already felt in his eyes and bosom, how could it be otherwise.

🔯

My grandfathers were no such successes as Abraham, although they too were wanderers. One grandfather always sat on a hard wooden chair next to an upright piano which nobody played. When I came into the apartment he never spoke but he gripped my arms and smiled at me with so much joy that it was like looking through the windows of a mansion aflame with light. Where the smile came from, since his wife sternly commanded and his sons embarrassedly ignored him, I did not know. There was a story my mother told me. When this grandfather was a young man in the old country, the police came to his house looking for pamphlets. A neighbor girl visiting his mama slipped the pamphlets from his room under her coat, ran home and hid them inside her own bed where the police never thought to search when they came to her house, where they never found the Marx and Bakunin, the sentences of broken chains. She took the risk because she was in love with him. So he married the girl—it was my grandmother—and brought her to America where he sewed fur coats on Canal Street for forty years. Only it had been her sister he was in love with. My mother said he felt it his duty to marry the one who saved his life. A year later the sister, too, came to Brooklyn, and visited them. A stormy scene. The sister was banished to Chicago, never to return, my grandmother never forgave anyone. That was why her voice was so sour, why she refused to travel in an automobile, why she always cooked too much food and forced us to eat it but was never seen eating anything herself, that was why my grandfather was not permitted to speak, and my uncles who lived at home had shifty eyes like prisoners. My grandfather sat like a poor guest in the corner, but I understood that whenever I stood before him I would receive, instead of words, the same astonishing ecstatic smile from the face with its yellowed teeth and pancake-size brown birthmark on the right, the same grip of the hard hands.

Look, everything is connected, a single universe means a single creator, of heaven and earth, light and shadow, sun moon stars, and on down to the sheep and mice. And all their movements. Then it follows, it's completely logical, the unity of God means the brotherhood of his creatures. The ethics branches from the metaphysics. For how is bread good when it rises? Good inside, good to eat, nourishment for others. To understand this simple fact is already to live in peace with your wife and neighbors, already to be blessed. How could it be otherwise. You rejoice in the wife of your bosom, since how can the man be happy without the woman's happiness. You give with a generous hand, seeing that the poor man is your brother. You avoid violence, which is the delight of the ignorant and beastly man but the dismay of the wise. For a lion cannot avoid violence, which is its nature, but a man can always negotiate. Of course, with God too. Why not? When the Holy One speaks with you he also listens. Or did you think he had a mouth but no ears?

All this Abram explains to his wife, who is famous for her beauty, though barren. They are in a valley, it's noontime, their people and animals are asleep, the cliffs bleached, a line of willows along a wadi traces a green stripe, a patch of purple lupine sprouts near their tent-peg. His wife curls and stretches her toes, her toenails she paints like ten pomegranate seeds, she rubs one of her amulets. Why is she barren, why bare? Because birth belongs to the Father.[†] The Mother whom Sarai foolishly worships does not exist, the Great Goddess does not exist. Asherah, Queen of Heaven, Lady of the High Places, Mother of all the gods, does not exist. The Holy One opens or closes a woman's womb. Forget your superstitions, throw away your

---

[†] In the next two generations Rebecca and Rachel also suffer barrenness, in order to remind us that God, not a fertility goddess, is responsible for building up the house of Israel. Or to put this another way, the Hebrew God

worthless idols, he tells her. Wood cannot see, stone cannot hear, statues cannot act. Think about it and be logical.

Then she bites him. He has to laugh, bite her back—right on the belly—they wrestle like puppies. Above them the sun sails. They creep into the tent where he sucks her nipples.

📖

My other grandfather walked across Europe from Byalistok, my mother tells me, carrying a suitcase of books. Pushkin, Schlegel, Heine, Shakespeare, Tolstoy, along with the medical texts, having discarded his study of Talmud. She tells how he nearly died of starvation, in London and New York. He worked fourteen hour shifts at the looms while studying at Columbia, attended meetings whose goal was to create the worker's paradise, and secretly ate the scraps his landlady left in the alley for the cats. It is this grandfather who a hundred times has told me the Story of the Man Who Traveled From Place to Place, full of encounters with fox and wolf, deep forest and sly peasant, rooster and whale, at the end of which he finds himself mysteriously on his own doorsill. He winks at me over the chessboard, the druggist playing with the doctor, two bald men in cardigans, their heads crowned by

---

appropriates the powers of the female deities he replaces. Mary Callaway traces the "barren mother" image from the matriarchs to the post-exilic period. Savina Teubal proposes that Sarah is represented as having sacred status: Mesopotamian priestesses were exempt from motherhood. An interesting further possibility is that Abram and Sarai derive from the Vedic Brahma and Sarasvati. Brahma is the Father-god or demiurge of Vedic Hinduism; Sarasvati is the goddess who caused language to come into being and invented art, music and poetry.

pipe smoke. Since there was no money he became a pharmacist
instead of a doctor, but when a customer cannot pay for a
doctor, my grandfather takes him in the back room and treats
him for free. After years of hunger he fails to collect the
overdue bills at the pharmacy, he worries that his customers
are poor people, he stoops, he hangs his head and strokes his
white mustache when my grandmother scolds.

🦎

She wants to know what the voice of God is like.

The voice is like the language of rock
The voice is frilled at the edges like a medusa
The voice is folded and folded like fabric
It is warm and salt
like tears—
It sounds like bells of cattle, his own herd,
        browsing on a nearby slope—

It sounds like his own voice.

Yet it fools Abram every time. He startles and looks around for
whoever is addressing him, then remembers and says *Here am*
I, as is proper. He cannot help smiling to himself shyly, so lifted
with happiness that God is visiting him. Then he cries, sometimes. For a concept of God is one thing but a living God is
another.

He has to be educated slowly. He travels from place to place
and lives in courts. Down to Egypt and up again. Sarai enables
him to be welcomed by Pharaoh, and later by Abimelech, who

load him with gifts on her account.[†] He grows prosperous in flocks, herds, oxen, gold, silver, menservants and maidservants. He makes a separation between his brother's son Lot and himself, when their flocks, herds, tents, and herdsmen become too numerous to be sustained peaceably in a single area. There is enough land for us both, he says; if you take the left hand I will take the right, and if you take the right hand, then I will go left. He goes briefly to war when Lot and his people are taken prisoner in a war between two sets of kings, but when the combat is over and his people are saved he refuses to accept booty: not a thread nor a shoe-latchet, lest his erstwhile allies claim they have enriched him. He respects the property of others, makes friends with his suspicious neighbors. On all matters of real estate, he negotiates. He is a man of peace, he represents the arts of peace, the diplomacy required to perpetuate a relationship, the avoidance of trouble before it begins, the reluctance to turn friction into violence. In the next three generations the same will be true of Isaac, Jacob, and Joseph. Bursting with seed, they will be fathers and family men. Not one of them will be a warrior.

He spends his middle years traveling, a trader, a dealer in camels, carpets, cattle, finally settling down. A man whose handshake you trust, still childless. His cows calve, sheep produce lambs, babies leap out of the servants. He dreams: a

---

[†] The repeated story of the patriarch who asks his wife to identify herself as his sister in the foreign court, so that the ruler who takes her will not kill him (Genesis 12:10–20, 20:1–18, 26:6–16), has been the subject of extended moral debate. There is no indication in the biblical text, however, that either Abram or Isaac is blameworthy in making his wife available to a ruler or in asking her to lie to save his life; in each case violence is avoided, God intervenes to protect the wife (the husband's property), and the husband is enriched.

curly-haired youth walks with him along a steep mountain trail.
Something happens, a noise, a rockslide in the ravine, and a
young ram dashes away over a slope, kicking up dust. They
race after the animal. He sees the boy leaping on the mountain,
hears his shout, he slows to a trot. The air is like lightshafts
falling through a forest, it seems very peaceful. Pungent, if
pungence is possible in a dream wilderness, with the redolence
of sage. Soon the boy appears far below, carrying the sheep in
his arms, that's the whole dream.

Eventually Abram's wife tells him to take her handmaid Hagar
the Egyptian. If children are born they will legally belong to
the wife, taking away her shame, that is what she decides she
wishes. She looks at him like a carpenter with a mouthful of
nails. So now at the age of eighty-seven he has a son. And the
spectacle of female jealousy. You're killing me, yells the wife.
She's killing me, yells the other one. It appears that the bread of
blessing, when one bites it, contains a stone. Sarai tells Abram
everything is his fault. Can it be? He tells her to do what she
wants with the girl, she beats her, the girl runs away, comes
back quiet. A temporary peace. Now with one eye Abram scans
a swarm of gnats, wildflowers casting their shadows, clouds
flying overhead. Yes, all is connected. The other eye watches
the women. His hands need to touch God, the way a house
needs its owner, its inhabitant, to lay a hand on its doorframe,
but there is still only a voice.

🔲

*My mother tells me this story of her grandfather, a man
she never met, a tzaddik revered for his tender heart. He
owned a thriving tanning factory with another man, and
when his partner died, her grandfather vowed to take care of*

*the man's young son. So when the factory caught fire my
great-grandfather made an announcement. The half that
burned down was his, he said; the unburned half belonged to
the boy. My great-grandfather became, officially, the child's
employee. But when the boy grew up he married a faithless
and greedy woman who demanded that he fire the old man.
She nagged until he agreed. The town was shocked, and my
great-grandfather went to the rabbi of Grodno for judgment.
When he explained his case, the great rabbi decided indig-
nantly in his favor. But my great-grandfather wished only
vindication before God, not revenge. He never returned to the
factory, his heart remained broken forever, he died in poverty.
My mother's eyes fill with East European moisture when she
tells this story. To be a tzaddik is to be innocent, righteous,
holy. But I am angry, I am an American, I think why sacrifice, why martyrdom, what about his wife and children.*

▧

When he is ninety-nine the Holy One appears in person. Suddenly, out of the blue. The invisible creator of the universe,
who gilds the sun, empurples the sky, and dries the earth in the
midst of many waters, imagine it, materializes into the form of
a man. He looks like Abram of course, an elderly herdsman
with a polished head and streaky beard. He tells his personal
name, El Shaddai, which means God-of-the-Breast-Hill-Moun-
tain.[†] Abram exults. Walk in front of me and be perfect, God
says, just as I am perfect. Teasing as he so often does, for the

---

[†] Exodus 6:3 tells us that Jahweh appeared not only to Abraham but also
to Isaac and Jacob as El Shaddai. The usual English rendering of this epithet
is "Almighty God" but the term is related to the Akkadian *sadu*, mountain,
and to the Hebrew *shad*, breast, so that El Shaddai may be a biogeological

body of an old man is far from perfect, it is full of aches and pains, Abram by now suffers from rheumatoid arthritis. Then he gives the new name: no longer Abram the exalted father, but Abraham the father of a multitude of nations. He announces an everlasting covenant, of which the visible sign is circumcision.

Now his voice is like a cold sky with high clouds. Explain covenant, Abraham murmurs. Like a contract, says the Holy One, only larger, more binding. Binding for many generations—in fact, forever. We have a task, he explains. The bodies of our men must recognize each other until the end of the world. And he quickly promises Abraham a son with his elderly wife, whose name also changes, from Sarai or princess, to Sarah, she who strives. Abraham falls on his face laughing, begs him to care for Ishmael, and Shaddai agrees, and disappears. Leaves only a few prints in the sand. That same day Abraham cuts the foreskin from Ishmael, the other men of his house, and himself, with his own hand. They bleed like women. They inhale the metallic scent of blood.

Abraham reconsiders the meaning of blessing. Now he understands that blessing is the pathway of learning, and that it is like a trail down a mountainside covered with thornbushes, so steep it seems bottomless, even at noon painted with sunlight.

Soon afterward three men approach Abraham's tent on a hot day. He rushes to offer them hospitality: cakes, butter, milk, the meat of a tender calf, the shade of a tree under which to commune.

---

pun like the "Grand Tetons." The term Shaddai alone is used in "poetic" portions of Isaiah, Ezekiel, Joel, Psalms, Job (where it appears 31 times), and Ruth 1:20-21.

One of the men turns out to be the Holy One, in the form of a traveler. He tells Abraham that his wife Sarah will bear a son within a year. Abraham is delighted but can hardly believe it; neither can Sarah, who is decades past menopause, but is anything too difficult for God? Then the Holy One waves the other two men away and takes Abraham aside. He confides that he plans to destroy two wicked cities, Sodom and Gomorrah. At this Abraham is distressed. Must not the judge of the whole world do justice, he asks. What if there are some good people in those cities? Is it right to destroy them? Do you want your enemies to defame you? The creator stands before him in a man's form; he is aware that he is arguing with the law of the universe itself. But the creator is also Abraham's friend, they have an agreement, a covenant, Abraham feels an obligation to advise him. He must say what is in his heart. That, too, is a law of the universe.

Is Abraham so simple that he thinks the Holy One, the El Shaddai, blessed be he, is a man like himself? No and yes. Is the universe, may it be praised, infinite and eternal? Well, then so is God infinite and eternal, Abraham reasons. But is he, Abraham, dust and ashes, a definite portion of the universe? Aha, and so God is also a man resembling himself.

But he argues with him?—And with whom better should he argue? So his reasoning concludes. He points out to God that the innocent should not suffer with the guilty. God appears pleased, so Abraham pursues the matter. Not for nothing has he spent time in marketplaces. If there are fifty without sin in the city will you save it? God agrees to this. What if there are only forty-five? Forty? Don't be angry, I'm only dust and ashes, a nothing, but what if there are thirty good people? God agrees

THE FATHERS I ☒ 61

to save it for thirty. In sum, he bargains God down to ten, which he believes will be sufficient.

☒

The next morning Abraham watches the smoke go up from Sodom and Gomorrah like smoke from a furnace. The sight makes him feel old, aggravates his arthritis, troubles his heart, gives him a whisper of angina. The pity of it, the pity of it. Eastward the sky turns a dirty tangerine, a rusted red, a rotted ash color, it is filled with splinters of bone.

For many days the bad color remains in the air, the wind carries the mingled smells of sulphur and of burned skin and hair, and then it goes away, and Abraham continues his life as a shepherd on the slopes above the plain.

☒

His second son is born, a honey of a boy, the triumph of his lifetime, Sarah's triumph also. No more wooden goddesses and barrenness, God has finally visited her. They invite hundreds of guests to the circumcision feast, she insists on nursing all the infants. At the weaning feast she sits like a queen. Viewing the mockery of Ishmael her stepson and Hagar her bondwoman she demands that Abraham cast them out. Abraham is reluctant, for he loves both his sons, but the Holy One tells him to obey his wife. Ishmael doesn't go very far in fact, they stay in touch, God takes care of him. But for Abraham the joy of old age becomes Isaac. And Isaac grows, straight as an arrow, strong as a young cedar, sweet as well-water.

When Isaac was nine years old the Holy One told Abraham to take the child on a three day journey and sacrifice him on Mount Moriah.

What could Abraham answer? The voice came from the hills, but as if the hills were smitten by a storm, buried in clouds. It was like a lightning crack in the storm. It struck Abraham like a mallet striking an ox. In this way he discovered his weakness, that he was actually beginning to die, and that the Holy One would die along with him. As one deteriorates, so the other. Fear nudged him like a dog's nose. And there was little Isaac. Isaac, his mother's darling. That sweetheart of a child. Isaac who would scamper among sheep, who would cry one minute and laugh the next. Who liked to run off and hide, then skim under his mother's armpit, then go off jumping. Frisky, alive, and the picture of health.

All the way to Moriah Abraham shivers. Woe overwhelms him, will braces him. He is stretching, stretching, and between the woe and the will it is as if teeth approach. Sharp teeth prepared to bite. There is no voice. But in heaven God too feels fear and trembling. So he sets the ram in the shrub—its horns tangled by branches—as a substitute, and sends the angel to shout when Abraham lifts the knife: *Touch not the child, neither do anything to him.*

It is in time, it is almost too late, it is better late than never.

> A father desires to murder his son
> murder his son
> murder his son
> A father means to murder his son
> and blessed be he
> who withdraws the hand of destruction

Afterward Abraham holds the boy to his bosom, thinking: We have bound him and freed him. He is ours. He belongs to us.

🌣

From the sacrifice of humans to the sacrifice of beasts: it is a momentous change, difficult for men to make, even more difficult probably for gods to make. Almost as difficult as to say, later, Thou shalt not kill. Imagine how the men, the gods, the civilizations must often feel yearnings for the crude old times, when they simply killed and killed. Imagine the subtle recognition that the desire to kill is natural, and that one may nonetheless refrain from killing. Imagine that moment, approaching murder, which we all may bloodily desire, under the skin of our kindness; that delight of the raised knife; then the renunciation, even at the last possible moment; the turning toward life.[†]

With a sigh, I think it—the turning toward life—for the story of Abraham at the same time records a dual triumph of the Father over the Mother. First the Holy One appropriates the

---

[†] The substitution of animal for human sacrifice, central to Judaism, may have been incomplete even in prophetic times: cf. Isaiah's anger at "You who burn with lust among the oaks, under every green tree; who slay your children in the valleys, under the clefts of the rocks," Jeremiah's cry that "They have built the high places of Topheth, which is in the valley of the sons of Hinnom, to burn their sons and daughters in the fire; which I did not command, neither did it come into my mind," and Ezekiel's accusation, "When you offer your gifts and sacrifice your children by fire, you defile yourselves with all your idols unto this day." In Psalm 106, "They sacrificed their sons and their daughters to the demons. They poured out innocent blood, the blood of their sons and daughters, whom they sacrificed to the idols of Canaan; and the land was polluted with blood."

power of a woman's womb, then he takes the power of the umbilical cord. Instead of flesh, a living pipeline, it becomes dead rope. It ties the child up, hand and foot. Where was Sarah when Abraham took his son up the mountain? The akedah, the binding of Isaac to God's altar, is the death of mother-right; it binds the boy to the theocentric world of the fathers.

That is not what the sages say. They explain that God is testing Abraham, God wants to see if Abraham will obey, God wants Abraham to be willing to sacrifice what he most loves. But there is also a problem here. Why does the creator of heaven and earth require us to submit to him, why does he wish to test us, what is the point of being worshipped, of being obeyed. Of proving one's dominance—I am God, I am God—again and again.

I want my grandfathers—men who were tender as butter—to show me, please, show me how one can love such a being!

How wide the bosom of Abraham, in which this complicated monotheism is born, which compels me to believe, which compels me to inquire.

❧

Unjust. I know it. My wife also knows it. She says nothing but she grows smaller and smaller, like a withered apple forgotten in the cellar. By the time she is ready to die she is quite dry and juiceless. When she dies I bury her in the cave of Machpelah, at the edge of a field, which I pay for with money. Here, eventually, they can bury me also. My long bones they will arrange beside her bones. So I ask myself, shaking my head sadly: Abraham, Abraham, after this can you still love God? Or maybe it's the Holy One himself, whispering mischievously: *Abraham, do you still love me?* Well, I say, that's a hard one but I confess I do. Maybe not with such a whole heart as before—you know very well my heart is broken—but as well as I can. To my dying breath. Tell me, do I have an option? Is there maybe another universe around the corner? Can you show me some other God to adore, some other Lord and King and Eternal and Infinite One?

As to the boy: he lives, he survives, it is enough. He too is captured. Tangled in God like the ram in the thicket. He too is blessed. He too will be a blessing.

🖾

She combs and braids my hair before I go to school. The fiber twists and tumbles, alive, alive, like inchworms. I am the only daughter of an only daughter. She was the wildflower, the tomboy, and the poet. The stories are mine because she tells them, braiding. She remembers after I was born, she would catch her father sneaking into my room. Papa, you should let the baby sleep, she would say. He pretended he had to go to the toilet, he would get up from the supper table, slip down the hall. She always found him leaning over my crib, singing in Yiddish, in the semi-darkness.

Sarah, or Defiance

Therefore Sarah laughed within herself, saying,
After I am waxed old shall I have pleasure,
my lord being old also?
GENESIS 18:12

You are entering the realm of the Mothers.
GOETHE

*H*ere he is again: wearing out the carpet of my tent, frowning, trying not to look at my face, frowning harder when I smile. He commands me to forget my idolatry. When I travel with him I must bring neither snake nor staff nor fruit, neither bangle nor ointment, nor prayer to the sacred vulva of the Mother. I must throw away my goddess figurines. An image cannot be fertile, cannot guarantee fertility, it is not alive. The Holy One is the Living God, all other gods are unreal. And so on. His eyes burn. A holy man with a holy theory. I like that about him. Still, I touch my own breasts, cup my own belly under my palm, feel for myself that my body is entirely alive. Sufficiently alive. I brush my hair over my polished bronze shoulder, I wait for him to finish his explanation.

And he goes in to Hagar
And I want to die

And she conceives
And is faithless to me
And mocks me
In front of him
Ignorant, servile girl
We should be allies
We are both exiles, all
Women are exiles
I tell her
She smiles slyly
And he is happy with her
And I want to die
And then it is my turn
Behold the fruit of my womb
Get out, I say
And take your snotnose son with you
God has blessed me
And my husband
Does what I tell him

▧

—Until he betrays me. He takes the boy without my permission. They are already gone when I wake and stare down the stony road into the haze of the rising morning. Birds shoot from the rocks, the sun clears the amber cliffs, it will be a hot dry one. I sniff the stirred-up dust. I crack my knuckles. I imagine bandits, a mountain lion asleep on a ridge, from a shadowless thistle at noon a snake suddenly striking. The old man useless. Impractical. The child defenseless, his slender thigh swollen, glazed like candy by fever. I am still thinking such thoughts when the sun drops toward the town of Beersheba

and again as it rises from the rocks, coating the mountaintops in
a bloody paint. I picture the congregation of vultures flapping
down from some broad limb, crowding around their discovery
like housewives at the butcher. Whoever lays a hand on my
child, I think, I'll kill him. Then I remember that I am powerless.

▧

I did not die of heartbreak
When my son was stolen
Or of joy at his return
Or of anger at my husband's God
Despite what you may have heard
When I died of age
He shut me in a box
I am but a stranger and sojourner
Among you, he said to the men of Hebron
It was the same story
When he exchanged me
For cattle and servants
With Pharaoh and Abimelech
Everyone pretending I was his sister
Though nobody was fooled

They bow and smile, the men
From the Hebron marketplace
They say: we will give you
A place to bury your dead
My husband is nervous, he pulls
At his wispy beard

He replies: give me
A place to bury my dead
Out of my sight—
He agrees to pay
An extravagant price, he
Senses me through wood, rock,
Gravel, grass,
Watching him.

And at last I put away my disguise, along with my skin, and join your own thought, to speak to you directly. Pay attention, women, it is a question of intelligence. We know that when a boy is bound to the fathers, to Our Father who claims to have no Mother, a portion of his mind snaps closed. Like someone condemned to a life sentence, he bows his head in its delicate cup of bone, he lets himself be cast into prison. Now nothing can ever enter or leave again, existence beats hopelessly against the valves of his fear anger disbelief. That is why men are unable to think clearly. They become heroes, shadows, a chain gang joined at the ankles, they follow the leader, they convince themselves they belong together. So? A bull can believe he created the meadow, a rooster can think he's singing.

There is a binding stronger than rope. I know it, you know, everybody knows. The boy loves his mother. Tender, radiant, needs another. Something milky in him, a secret, delicious and big, so juicy he has to forget it. Do you know what we give the man who enters our body? Do you know what we give the child who suckles us? When a baby clings to our neck, smells our sweating and tastes us, when we laugh in the baby's face, or the man's arms, do you know the instruction we transmit? A spill, a spiel, a spool, the message in the milk, the kind account of the cunt, cuneiform. Conundrum. They cannot erase our joy from their flesh, to the last generation, and for this reason we can lose battle after battle, suffering staggering losses, yet continue to be winning the war. Life against death. Women, haven't you noticed we're winning it?

The Opinion of Hagar

And Sarah saw the son of Hagar the
Egyptian, which she had born unto
Abraham, mocking. Wherefore she said
unto Abraham, Cast out this bondwoman and
her son: for the son of this bondwoman shall not be
heir with my son, even Isaac.
GENESIS 21:9–10

And the living nations wait,
Each sequestered in its hate.
W. H. AUDEN

I have no opinion
I am an Egyptian woman
They sold me and made me her slave
Like everyone else I was in love
With her beauty
She pretended to care for me
Forget about our nationalities, forget
About social rank, she would say
We are women together
That is what matters, Hagar

She used me
When she couldn't have a child herself
She made me sleep with her husband
—That old, creepy man—

When my son was born
She was yellow with jealousy
Of my round breasts, of my strong healthy boy
Finally she too had a son
What a laugh, a thin stick of a baby
Who whined and spit up his food all day
Just what you would expect
From those threadbare sacks of parents
But that was the end of me
She threw me away
Like garbage

Hagar, she jeered, Hagar the stranger

You see how humble I am
My son is another story[†]
Not like me, he is free and courageous
A wild ass of a man
He can read and write
He can run a printing press
He can shoot an AK-47
I call him Ishmael, I whisper to him:
Fight to your dying breath

But I still wonder
Why could she not love me
We were women together

[†]According to tradition, Isaac is the ancestor of the Hebrews, Ishmael the ancestor of the Arabs. In the Koran, it is Ishmael (Ismail), not Isaac, who is almost sacrificed by Abraham (Ibrahim).

The Cave

Come, let us make our father drink wine,
and we will lie with him, that we may
preserve the seed of the father.
GENESIS 19:32

Cave girl mama
Don't you go down on me.
Oh cave girl mama
Don't you go down on me.
Take your pretty legs and your tangled hair
Away and just leave me be.

What is a cave, and how deep must it go, they must have wondered. The girls, they were really women, the daughters, the daughters of their father. They had never known a man. You remember the daughters. The first important ones. Daughters of Lot, nieces of Abraham, temporary inhabitants of Sodom, a city of the plain which is no longer in existence. They themselves had not looked back, unlike their mother. Unlike, unlike. Unlike who? Long afterward they might have hung on a ledge, peering, back there, at the widths of the flat landscape, so difficult really to discern anything, a mineral formation, back there, a mineral formation in the middle of what was flat and burnt-out, really, standing up it could have been white and salty, it could have been shaped like a pillar, only it was difficult, really, to see anything.

The hawks, they spiral. I wish I could be like them. Blindingly cruel, the floating, on the airdrafts, far below one's feet, gradually ascending until you can distinguish the feathers at the wing-ends dipping, lightly, to steer them. Now time goes by, I'm hypnotized by the breeze. And then when they drop, it is just like a thunderbolt, the talons come out, the beak widens, it is over in a minute. The killing is over in a minute, a swift crunch, a swallow, and the gliding begins again, the volumes of space, the shadowy cliffs, the hypnosis.

A holocaust is unlike this. Unlike, unlike. For example, it takes much longer. It is much louder. It stinks worse. It is much more redness. Far, far more redness. (How do the girls know, if they don't see it? If they obey and don't look back? They still know. How could they fail to know. Perhaps they know by the heat, perhaps by the roar. For everyone has heard a fire roaring, and felt the terrifying heat when you come too close, that whips at your back even when you are running away, until you are finally to freshness). While you are running away it is going on, on, on.

Afterward the smoke of the country goes up like smoke from a furnace.

A cave mouth. You go inside the mouth, it becomes cool, it can be comfortable, it can be home. Deep in, here you are, fix it up, girls. You have to be hiding. You have to keep on hiding here. But why?

They were wicked people. But is it true that the girls can never go back, can never in fact leave these cliffs where they are hiding out, and this cave here? The cities were all full of wicked people, so the girls must not (they do not) remember the girls who used to be their friends, or the mothers of those girls. They must not (do not) think about their clothing, their jewelry, or their makeup. Bad girls. Bad mothers. Now they are cinders.

Innocence means: we have never known a man. Father says: we are good girls. He tries to pet our heads but his hand slides over the fronts of our faces. It is like having a blind person touch you. He cries all of the time. It is disgusting.

Innocence means: we do not remember the night the two men were staying at our house, the night the drunken crowd was roaring outside our door (we used to see them in daytime, our girlfriends' fathers, brothers, and uncles) banging at the windows (wanting to fuck our visitors), the night our father took us by the elbows and tried to push us outside the door instead. He thought we might be a substitute, and yelled through the door that they should do whatever they wanted with us. He was pulling one way, we were pulling the other, screaming our heads off. Our mother was screaming, hitting him, trying to get his face with her nails. Innocence means we do not remember our mother.

Here we are in the cave. Cool and nice, cool and safe. Some of the rocks look like dragons and some like camels, we eat over here and we sleep over here, using skins. But he cries all of the time and it is disgusting. Tears and snot and dribble mingling on his face. We ask him about husbands. Where is he going to find us husbands, because we have to have children. But he dribbles and bawls, and it is really disgusting. Also he gets drunk every night.

It is easy to get him drunk.

Now it is easy, when he is drunk and asleep. We are giggling for days beforehand. You go first. No, you.

Oily, I've used the fat of a wildcat I skinned. Candle steady, shadows on his nipples he's sound asleep, I can look him over head to knees. Unlike, unlike. Unlike ourselves, less soft but more meaty. I circle the dove brown aureoles with my index finger, skim lightly by the hairs until the nipples harden like snaps. I use my tongue tip and, very carefully, my teeth. I crouch until my breasts flap against his face like hot towels. The air grows denser and the room heats from the single candle's brilliant orange cone, edged gold, diffused to smoke lifted like a string. His red body resembles clay which invites the fingers to burrow in. I pursue the rivulets of his fur down the center, downstream, I make it wet and greasy, I make it shine. Now here is his baby thing, a sleepy puppy. Now here we go, a dog sitting up begging. Oh my mama I'm happy filling up my mouth with figs, another breast, the blissful childhood I can't remember. And slip now and slide. Mama, no giggling. A gush of blood, but it feels good. God, it feels finally good.

First me then her. Tomorrow her then me.

Do you guess he was only pretending to be asleep, on the ledge, the skins, the leaves, in the warm room in the cave.

❧

> Cave Girl Mama
> Go put your red dress on
> Yeah Cave Girl Mama

Go put your red dress on
Put some lipstick on your mouth and we'll
Cakewalk into town.

Isaac, or Laughter

Two Jews are in prison, about to be executed.
Brought before the firing squad, the first one asks
the guard: Officer, could we have blindfolds?
The second turns to his friend and whispers:
Sh, don't make trouble.
THE SHORTEST JEWISH JOKE

My name is Laughter, and I laughed
Knowing everything's absurd.
For God in his ironic craft
Made all more and less than his word.
IRVING FELDMAN, "WORKS AND DAYS"

So I was telling you this story about my father, right? So it's a joke. So I'm a comedian, sue me, named Isaac, or laughter, or Ikey, or maybe kike, since before the foundations of the world. Well, at least since before my mother's womb, just a little before, you know that story? The old dad, he's a hundred already, and the old mom—she's not a mom, this is the problem, she's ninety and there's nothing. All these years she's been following the old man around, she traipses from Ur to Canaan, and from Canaan to Egypt, and from Egypt back to Canaan, she pretends to be his sister, this, that. And nothing. No child. No beautiful little baby she should hold it, she could tickle it under the chubby double chin, she could wipe the baby drool, she could have some pride already the way a woman needs to. A good family she comes from, they're fertile as goats, but not my mother, she's barren. And she's a little bitter. Not at my father, no. He is kindness itself to her, never a rebuke, much less a blow, God forbid he should strike her, a good and loyal woman. It's God she's bitter at, who has been making promises but not keeping.

Go here, go there, God has been telling her husband. Listen, I'm your friend, I wouldn't steer you wrong. This land I'm going to give you—it's fantastic. The Tigris, the Euphrates— listen to me. Egypt move over. So big, so sweet this land—you won't regret it. Such a land, a land of brooks of water, of fountains and depths that spring out of valleys and hills. A land of wheat and barley, and vines, and fig trees, and pomegranates; a land of oil, of olive and honey. A land wherein you shall eat bread without scarceness, you shall not lack anything in it. You like this picture? It's yours. And what I'm telling you—are you listening carefully?—is that you are going to have this sweetness, this milk and honey, not only for yourself but for your descendants, who will be as numberless as the sands of the seashore and the stars of heaven. Children are the least of your worries.

My father of course would listen. A trusting man. A good man. To the bone, my father: good. Perhaps a little too trusting, my mother would think, but it wasn't him she blamed. In fact, seeing he was discouraged and confused as he got along in years, she actually gave him her own handmaid to sleep with, which is how my father's first son, my half-brother Ishmael, came into the world. So then the old man was happy, and the old woman—not so happy. Because now her handmaid was looking at my mother with pity and even contempt. My mother isn't my mother yet, of course, you understand. She's still barren. She has nothing. Now not even her pride. And what is she? She's ninety. An old lady. Her skin is burned dry and brown from the sun, like leather. She has begun to shrink up. Soon she will be gathered to her mothers and it will be as if she never existed on the earth.

And she can't blame her husband.

Now imagine this. One fine day the old man is sitting in our tent door when he sees three travelers approaching. He runs inside the tent for water to wash their feet, tells his wife quickly to make three cakes from her best flour, and gets a servant to prepare meat from a tender calf. So then the men are sitting under a tree having their meal, with the old man standing by, when the visitors ask where the wife is. Inside, he says. Which God knows is the truth. I mean she is right inside, the ear like a tape recorder at the tent flap, listening. So when the man announces to her husband that she is going to have a son, of course she hears it and starts to laugh inside herself. She's going to have pleasure like this at her age? After she hasn't had a period, even, for two decades, and the husband as well is stricken with age—is this ridiculous, or is it ridiculous? Mind you, she makes no more sound with her laughter than a bird makes flying. But God knows all, and asks the old man why his wife has laughed—does she think anything is too difficult for the Lord?—and repeats the announcement. At this point he peeks inside the tent. My mother, who is not yet my mother, denies that she laughed. No, says God, raising an eyebrow. You did laugh. And he goes away. Whether God is laughing or not, who knows? But in due time my mother conceives me, and when I am born you can well believe my mother is a happy woman. So that on the day of my circumcision she is laughing all day, only now it is out loud. For, says she, who would have told my husband that I, at my age, would bear him a child? And look at me. I'm nursing a son. To everyone at the party she says God has made her laugh so that whoever hears it will laugh with her. It's a very joyous day and this is how I obtained my name.

But the story I'm telling you concerns my father, and it is even funnier. I've already explained the kind of man my father was. Kind and trusting. A very gentle person. Tall, fair-skinned, hands as wide as hawk's wings. You know how certain tall stooping men are full of good intentions but their heads are somewhere over the rainbow? Of course he had this long-standing relationship with God, which would explain a great deal in his character. Or if you look at it the other way, in all likelihood God picked him precisely for his trusting nature. Either way, they had a long, rich friendship. When I was a small boy he was forever telling stories about their many meetings, how God had said do this and do that, and how well it had turned out. Didn't we have so many and so many goats, sheep, calves, and so on? Weren't we promised the length and breadth of this beautiful land for our future seed?

Of course I had not seen this God myself, but you would never doubt a man like my father. The most you could complain would be that he might talk the feathers off a chicken, the same stories again and again, without a thought to whether the listener was genuinely entertained or, to tell the truth, without caring all that much who the listener might be. Usually it was my mother and myself. But when he would talk you would listen anyway, even if you heard it a million times before. My mother might give me a little tickle or pinch when he got started, or she might wink at me and suppress a smile. I would look at the thin white hair that waved around his dome when he was telling the exciting parts, as if it trembled with sympathy; and his forehead, that resembled hammered bronze; and his wide winglike hands, that would dance slowly alongside the story.

When he would finish a story he would beam at us. Funny he wasn't, but a lovely man. The innocence of him. I felt the awe a son feels for his father. But above and beyond, if this man would smile at you, you would feel as if all the angels loved you, such a sweetheart he was, such a shining would come from him.

And what happened? I'm nine years old, still a tender calf myself, the morning he wakes me to tell me we're going on a trip. The sun isn't even up yet, there's an ass saddled in front of the tent, some split firewood tied on, and two servants. He puts me on the saddle in front of him, and we're off. I promptly fall asleep. When I wake it's already mid-day. We're trotting along. The sun is beating down, no sign of shade is anywhere, I'm hungry and thirsty, my lips are cracked from dryness. I want to know what's happening, where we are going. The old man not only won't answer me, he won't look at me. He's looking off at the horizon somewhere to the side. Left side, right side, left side again. His right hand gripping me like iron, binding me against his body, but not a word. I'm totally mystified, right?

The servants won't talk either. One looks at his shadow in the sand, purses his lips together like a prune, and shakes his head when I try to get something out of him. The other jerks his head in the direction of the old man, like a wild ass trying to shake the reins off. The old man is pale as a snowcloud. He is so pale it's like a personal little snowfall around his head and hands, right?

I get the bright idea that my father is finally taking me to introduce me to God. Terrific. I feel very important. Nobody is talking, I figure, because he wants it to be a surprise.

On the third day we see a mountain, a purplish cone-shaped shadow, ahead of us. We leave the servants and the animal, my father straps the wood to my shoulders, and we start climbing. It's a relief because there are trees and bushes here, after the empty heat of the desert. I'm not even tired. In fact, I'm almost running up the trail, because I'm so excited. We stop at the top and it's gorgeous. Incredible. The shade and moisture around us, all the mixed smells and beyond us the entire world. With some scrambling over the rocks I can see a full circle of all the land around this mountain—mostly irregular hills, a tawny, yellowish-grey color, shading off at the horizon into a dusty brownish blue. The sky is an extremely vivid blue, but I can't tell where sky stops and earth starts. It's too bright. I can see the track we have come along, looking like a scratch running away from us. I can see other tracks, and dark patches of trees here and there where tracks meet.

Back under the trees I have trouble seeing at first with my dazzled eyes. My father is building an altar. He works fast. I ask where the lamb is for the offering, not really expecting him to answer since it is so long since I have heard his voice. He looks at me as if he too is dazed and says God will provide. Now I am totally excited, jumping like an oil drop in boiling water, ready to meet my father's God. I really, finally am going to meet him myself. And what happens?

The altar is finished. The old man ties me to it. He takes a knife out. Big enough to slit a sheep's throat. I can't believe this. My stomach drops. My body wants to curl up, but I can't move any part of myself except my feet, my fingers, and my head. My wrists and ankles are roped to the stone. I can feel every muscle contract, try to be smaller, my fingernails dig into my palms, my eyes closed as tight as I can close them, my face trying to become a small, small wrinkled raisin. In the middle of this, while I am unsure whether I am still alive or dead already, I hear a voice. The voice sounds as if the sky were speaking, it's very harmonious. It commands my father not to kill me. To be precise, it orders him not to lay a hand on me.[†] When I open my eyes what I see is my father leaning over me in an awkward position, chest hollowed and elbows stuck out sideways. He's struggling with my ropes, pulling at knots with his fingertips while trying not to touch my body. A funny sight if it were not so sad. His face looks like a bruised half-rotten peach, full of flushed blotches. Behind him, bushes and trees in all their soft, confused colors. Behind that, patches of the intensely bright sky, sticking from between the branches like the thin tines of a pitchfork. And in the shadow under a bush, a ram I didn't notice before, caught by its horns in some branches, yanking its head and looking very nervous.

[†] The midrash says that God sent an angel to speak to Abraham because he was too embarrassed to do so personally. But Abraham demanded God tell him himself; then demanded that God promise to forgive his children whenever they retell this tale. For this reason the Torah reading for Rosh Hashonah, which begins the Days of Awe, includes the Akedah.

Listening to a voice doesn't count as meeting someone. So I did not get to meet God as I expected. But neither did the old man.

The joke is that the old man never saw him again. After all those years of buddy-buddy, the agreements and the mutual heartfelt promises of eternal friendship—thin air. No more voices, not to mention comradely visits. No further instructions from On High. I'm here turns into I'm gone for good. Can we explain this? Did God perhaps discover he had pressing business elsewhere? Did he expect the old man to object when he was told to sacrifice me, just as he had objected when he heard about the plans for Sodom? Maybe God intended a replay. He would say, Sacrifice your son for me, and my father would say he knew God was only kidding, and they would slap each other on the back. Did he have any idea my father was going to be such a schlemiel? Who knows? Maybe the entire tale of friendship, promises, the land stretching from over here to over there, was an elaborate set-up. Believe it or not, some people have characters like this. They'll wait forever to pull a fast one, it amuses them. Not a bad joke on somebody, in any case. But whether or not God is laughing, that we don't know.

The Opinion of the Ram

And Abraham lifted up his eyes, and looked,
And behold behind him a ram caught in the
thicket by his horns.
GENESIS 22:13

The jackal whines when he is hungry,
every fool has folly enough for despondency,
and only the wise man can tear the veil of being
with his laughter.
ISAAC BABEL

*I*n Talmud it is said that he who humiliates another before the world shall lose his portion of paradise. Yet God humiliated Abraham before Isaac. And that was only the beginning. Think of the generations of pious Jews who trusted in God to rescue them from their enemies. Therefore, in my opinion, His only escape, and the reason He continues to reign in the world to come, is that Isaac forces himself to laugh, making light of this betrayal. Yes, Isaac knows that his father has been fooled and humiliated. But if he laughs at the entire world, treating it as absurdity top to bottom, including God, then God won't be punished, won't lose sovereignty. And if for a moment Isaac should cease to laugh, in that moment the universe would be annihilated.

Rebecca's Way

And they called Rebecca, and said unto her,
wilt thou go with this man? And she said,
I will go.
GENESIS 24:58

Imagine my joy at his whisper:
I'll never leave you, he said.
ANON., EGYPTIAN, CA. 1500 B.C.E.

It is written that he loved me,
That I consoled him
For his mother's loss.
They invented this concept,
Love, for the way a man
Gropes in the dark like an infant
With his please, please, please. . .
Like milk teeth tucked in the gums,
Like a fallen pear
Showing its indelible bruise.
It is written that he was blind,
That I made a fool of him,
That I reached into his testicles
Like someone thrusting a hand
Up to the elbow in a sack
Of slippery grain
And yanked those boys out

And made him bless
The smart one
Not the muddy hunter.
Right. I am Rebecca,
The boss, the balaboosta.
Dropping my veil and my skirt
I plant myself in the future.

It was sunset when I first saw him—
In the cool of the day
A man alone in a field
Far off, pink with grief.
As I jumped from my camel
Torn between excitement and pity
A lightning flash told me
This one will never get in your way.
God sends those flashes,
They raise my raven hair
Up from my head like wings
And squeeze my loins.
Girl, use your brain. I was never timid.
I was a strong girl at the well,
Well, well,
I went without hesitation
As it is written,
Hoping to do exactly what I did,
And now the chosen one
Jacob, my slippery son,
Will prevail with God and men, and will
Be Israel.

Jacob, or the Man of Touch

*And Jacob was left alone; and there wrestled a
man with him until the breaking of the day.*
GENESIS 32:24

*And before I discovered that my hard fathers
are soft on the inside, they died.
And all the generations that came before me are
many acrobats
mounted on one another in the circus,
and usually I am the one on the bottom
while all of them, a heavy load, stand on my
shoulders,
and sometimes I am on the top: one hand lifted
to the roof; and the applause in the arena below
Is my flesh and my reward.*
YEHUDAH AMICHAI

*T*he Times *has dropped into twilight disarray. Father and
son, at opposite ends of the sofa, have finished with it.
The younger man stretches ostentatiously, the older slumps.
They must decide what to do during the hour and a half
before dinner. They are both too irritable to listen to music.
The son goes to the window and leans out, staring at the
traffic and the miserable weather, the unfriendly city sky a
bilious tint of orange. They decide to play chess. The father is
thinking: I'll kill him. The tension in the father's midsection
is a dull expanding patch; for a couple of weeks he has worried*

there is an ulcer there. The father is thinking: I'm so tired,
I'm always so tired. They go to the bathroom to wash the
newsprint from their hands. First the son, then the father, steps
to the sink and rapidly soaps and rinses, and they do this
without brushing each other, both in their bluejeans.

The father is thinking: Let's go. The son is thinking: I'll kill
him. The father thinks: Mama's boy. Reader, this is a fiction.
I am a mama writing this fiction.

Jacob lies alone, not quite asleep, head on a flat, black stone. He
has come out from the camp where his wives, children, maidservants, and servants rest innocently in their tents. Between
them and himself flows the boundary of a small brook. The
night is warm, starry. The sneering camels have folded up their
legs like wooden furniture. Chair slats, large joints. Tough,
superior, they expect to outlive this present company. They
have grouped themselves for the night like old veterans, survi-
vors of decades of intermittent bloody slaughters, whose jokes
and stories primarily concern the defeated, their moments of
incaution, their spilled intestines, their picked red muscled flesh.
Chewing, drooling, the ropy thick lips of the camels are like
pistons, attached to bodies able to maneuver the wilderness like
armored tanks.

The backs of the sheep resemble a hilly island bathed in mild
starlight. Although too dirty and stupid to earn respect, and too
mean-tempered to solicit love—except when some child or
woman adopts a rejected twinned lamb—they are peculiarly
comforting creatures. To plunge hands and arms into their

fleece is for Jacob like the memory of his mother's fragrant embrace. The mother's hair, when she let it out, would slide in warm brown waves to her waist. He has tended flocks all his life, yet his eyelids still shut automatically when he touches a sheep's back, his anxieties dissolve the way stars melt at dawn. With his eyes closed and his fingers slipping through oily fleece, he can briefly forget the permanent smears under the animal's tail, and the sheep-eyes themselves snapping with fear. We are all like sheep, he thinks sorrowfully. Myself a runaway lamb, soiled and afraid.

The sand here is packed hard. The stars, like single grains, are staring down. The stone is not the same stone on which he pillowed his head during the journey out, twenty years ago, when as a cocky youngster he fled the hunter-brother whom he had outsmarted. The being that befriends him showed him the shining ladder and the remote ones ascending and descending. He doesn't forget that stripe of light, unearthly. Though it was long ago, he thinks possibly the picture will reappear with further instructions. He has wrapped himself in the same woolen cloth his mother first made him as a traveling coat, the one with the blue-dyed border and the fringes he used to slip his thumb and forefinger along.

The coat was lucky, so he has kept it. He has always trusted luck, though he is not a gambler. What Jacob's enemies say is that he is smart and charming, a tactician and a skillful bargainer. He admits it. He will also point out that he is extremely competent and scrupulously honest, at least since his youth, unlike some of the people he has to deal with. Since he is no fighter, no hot-head, he needs these qualities, the virtues suited to states of peace. But Jacob is convinced that luck is more essential to a man than any of his personal characteristics, which are after all merely a matter of the man's control. His character is as it were the work of his own hands. Luck is more like the breast a child sucks, the arms that hold him, something satisfyingly large and old. He likes to remind himself that the breast sometimes teases and removes itself but always reappears if you need it, that is after all its nature.

From Peniel it was no great distance to Edom. Redlands. Red and rude. By mid-morning he could expect to encounter Esau's army. Four hundred men. By his estimate he was outnumbered by approximately ten to one. The question was, in part, how angry Esau would still be. They had led their lives separately. Indeed, he had kept well out of Esau's way. The brother had materially prospered. The gifts sent ahead would conceivably help: two hundred female and twenty male goats, two hundred ewes and twenty rams, thirty she-camels with their colts, forty cows, ten bulls, twenty she-asses and their foals, sent drove by drove to Esau, not unimpressive.

Still, by noon tomorrow, Jacob's throat might be slit like a sheep's, and his blood already absorbed by the thirsty, hard-packed, warm brown sand, leaving only a stain of somewhat darker brown. All right. All right. And what of the women and boys. All of whom he has worked for by the sweat of his brow, and every one of whom he loves the way a girl loves a firstborn child, a heartache. Dangling beads to it, dressing it in embroidery, giving it suck and song. Seven years for the wall-eyed Leah who after all was the first and did her best. Then another seven years for Rachel, the nimbus and ecstasy of whose kisses he needed the way most men need money. Then all the years afterward mediating the competition between his two fierce wives—and their handmaids—making babies. He has cherished every one of them, it's what he was born for, and they trust him. On that account they may all die, following him.

Perfect silence. The cloth fringes. Tzitzit, locks of hair. One stroke. Two strokes. Three. The long smooth hair of the abandoned mother.

He lies with his eyes closed, waiting for a large light to open them: either the amazing stadium-floodlights that illuminated the ladder, or plain daylight. What he should do in fact is sleep, so as a practical man he relaxes. As he sleeps, then, no light. It will be a lengthy night. He breathes regularly, inside his blanket. Then a dim light, aureole, stroking his wrapped form, his naked face, giving no warmth. It's a flashlight or a swung lantern.

The blanket pulled, pulled off. He opens his eyes.

The newsprint from the Times *is smearing the wife's fingers, but she is working on the crossword. He claims men don't communicate with each other the way women do, thinks the wife. He thinks I don't understand. I understand all right, thinks the wife, pressing her lips together, wishing she could concentrate on the puzzle. He hardly ever hugged him or carried him when he was a baby. Wouldn't put his arm around him when he was a kid. When he hit puberty and was spending hours a day masturbating in the bathroom I said Talk to him privately but he never did it, not once. His own son. Now look at them, like a couple of pieces of frozen fish.*

🌒

Jacob is a short man, barrel-chested, narrow-hipped. His skin remains hairless, smooth as an oiled sculpture, in his manhood as in his youth, so that women when he is making love with them have always said, appreciatively: Ah, you're just like a boy. His legs are solid muscle, his feet small.

The other is the same. *But so beautiful,* thinks Jacob, as he opens his eyes and rises. *Unbelievable.* For this one is not shining, but the color of black olives. Or as if the sweet blackness of a night sky, while remaining arched above us—shadow in which the constellations are floating—were to condense at the same time into a man's form. His black hair plummets in a single braid down his back. His eyes are almond shaped, their pupils dark and their whites almost citron. Around his lips, wide and pink, flares a smile.

They stand naked except for their bound genitals. When they begin to wrestle, in the solemn darkness, under the stars, it is chest to chest like straining lovers. Joints grating, they try one grip then another. When they gasp the sound seems blunted by the warm air. Hearing would be impossible for the sleepers in the tents, even were Jacob to call for help, and he does not think of it. The low moans that they issue appear, again, not to ripple into the atmosphere but to fall at their feet. They themselves fall to the ground as they grapple.

Their sweat mingles, they slip and muddily slide against each other, the skin of each comes to appreciate the slippery volumes of the other. One chest feels the pounding of the other.

It is not like making love. Unlike, unlike. No orgasm, no release, no sperm. It is not like an ordinary fight. It is like being detained on an unknown charge by police in unfamiliar uniforms. The stars slide relentlessly across the sky and he does not see. Not to die, thinks Jacob, simply defend myself, try nothing risky. The large arm pressed around his throat, tightening, draperies of color begin to sway before Jacob's eyes as he starts to strangle, pivots from knees, throws arm off. The being staggers back, rushes forward like wind, flashes an openly sensual smile, seizes his leg and touches the hollow of his thigh, snaps the leg backward so that Jacob hears the crack, they slip and hit the sand together.

Color comes into the sand. It is brown, fawn, with a few scattered chips of whitish rock.

🔹

Years ago, they lifted weights. I need to keep in shape, the father would say, swallowing his dessert cheesecake, and I have no hour free in the middle of the day. Most days I even eat lunch at the office. Do you think the calls stop coming in? The father habitually uttered complaints that were also boasts, like the other successful men he knew. An unappealing habit which annoyed his wife, so he usually wished he'd bitten his tongue. Yet he always spoke no more and no less then the truth, as his wife well knew. He wished he knew what the boy thought. You could never tell. After the son's bar mitzvah the father wondered how long it would take the boy to become stronger than himself. At the son's fourteenth birthday party the father remarked that they might have a contest for the son's fifteenth birthday, and the boy shrugged.

It was not a question of whether but of when. The father had reached his peak strength at sixteen. The boy seemed softer than himself, a sissy, because the mother spoiled him. Treated him like a privileged child, some Jewish prince, like his farts didn't stink. Invisible fists deliver blows to a man's head when he thinks like that about his son. But you never could tell. Life is full of surprises. Theoretically they worked out every night when the homework was done, but in practice they did it maybe three times a week. Sometimes it was the father who reminded the son, sometimes the son who pressured the father.

On the son's fifteenth birthday, before dinner, they went to the parents' bedroom, where the weights were. They shut the door firmly behind them. The mother knocked and asked if she could come in, and the father said no.

🦪

So that he holds him. Color comes into the sand. Shadowless, with white scattered stones. So that the weight of his body lies on top of the body of the being. Jacob has pinned him, he is holding him, and he says let go, and his weight rests on him, would like to crush him, and he says let me go because the day is breaking. Can't move a thing. Thighs interlock, the face below him a shadow, a faint pink smile, he says let me go now.

To have defeated the being. He has defeated the being. Has he defeated the being, how can man defeat the being, how, he has actually done so, his weight is on him, his slippery body underneath is motionless, has he, is it a trick, or is it a true contest, the sand is shadowless, the face and the body below him a dark form, a smile, he cannot move, is it a trick, or is it a game, did I initiate it when I left my tent, or earlier, do we move back and forth alternately. Jacob is wondering all of this during the fraction of a pulsebeat in which we wonder things. Because it is a famous story, it is the climax of a play or game or trick. How can man defeat being unless the laws of being permit it. Everybody knows things so this is one of the things Jacob already knows, of course it is a game but he has to figure out his next move. He could ask, he could say: Promise not to kill me, promise I will not die in the morning.

A pain enters his chest darkly and spreads, as a calm darkens among water-lights of a lake. It spreads and reddens, it takes the form of a bearded man, whose left hand is running through his youthful curls in a gesture of perplexity, and whose right hand touches his chest in a gesture of surprising grace and delicacy, given that both chest and head are furry as an animal's. Brother, says the pain. Then it spreads and darkens further under him.

The pain shivers and is blind as a new lamb. An old man trembling in a bed. The loins look as if they have been in freezing water, shrunk and wrinkled, the skin hangs like a rotted fleece. Yet from these loins, from that pathetic brown bag of skin came Jacob. It is scarcely to be believed. It is a trick, he has tricked the old man, doing what his mother said, doing what she said, bringing in the meat the old man wants, the meat that the brother (the favorite) killed, wearing the brother's vest for the smell, wearing the hairy glove for the touch, and saying he was Esau, he has got it, haha he has tricked him, he has cheated him, the old man took the meat, smelled the clothing, petted the glove, and Jacob has got the blessing, Jacob is covered.

He is reaching his hand out, that the old man caresses feebly, the old man's blind eyes roll, the old man says the blessing, *my soul blesses you,* but Jacob's hand is covered, it does not feel anything, and anyway the old man is like dry sticks, dry bones. Jacob is so dark now, he is holding so hard. Is it a trick it is a trick. Dark but you reach. Pulled through, the sides so slick, pushed along, wetness then warmth, hold on, hold, like being in a tunnel, like being in a carwash, the rotating felt strips flapping at you as you are push-pulled forward, like being in a boat in a tunnel in an amusement park house, totally black, jerked along, strange screams, but you hold on, you jerk around a corner and there's a light slit, a horizontal stripe, and as you approach it opens and you are out, still holding onto your brother's heel, in the horrible light, in the cold light.

There is the faint smile, like a rift in shadow. Jacob is trying to read this smile, trying to think while his strength ebbs. He feels himself weakening, not only because of the nightlong struggle but because of the beauty of this body which every instant grows more absolutely dark as the dawn approaches. Not to die, he admonishes himself, ask not to die, fool, and then, as if you were to turn a corner of a city block and find yourself in a pasture—

Oh give me whatever is best for me, you must know what it is, whatever I took from my father by cheating and have earned now in honest fight, man against being, give it to me! give it to

me! give it to me!—Having paused for a pulsebeat Jacob's lips
open to whisper: *I will not let thee go except thou bless me.* As he
speaks the dawn breaks, a spear of fire shot into the world,
illuminating the theater of sand as if it were the hosts of heaven
applauding. Of course it is the hosts of heaven applauding,
what else would it be, they have all been cheerfully observing
the game, the game about playing.[†]

Now his brother, already advancing over the horizon with four
hundred men, is going to run to meet him. He will embrace
him, fall on his neck and kiss him; his face will be to Jacob like
God's face. For the other, to whom the exhausted Jacob has
spoken, is giving him a new name. He is no longer Jacob, akev/
heel. He will be Israel. Ish/man + sarah/to strive, + El/God.
Israel who prevails with God and man, and whose children will
be as the stars of the sky.

📧

The mother works on the puzzle. She hopes the son wins.
They are over there at the chessboard, concentrating
totally, in their bluejeans, by the window. She hopes the son

---

[†] The defeat of God by Man in the Jacob story anticipates the anecdote of
a Talmudic dispute between Rabbi Eleazer and Rabbi Joshua. God shows his
support of Eleazer by uprooting a carob tree, making a stream flow backward, letting the walls of the shul half topple, and a heavenly voice speak in
favor of Eleazer's opinion. But Rabbi Joshua who has the majority on his
side cites Deuteronomy 30:12, "It is not in heaven," which tells us that
Torah is here in our hearts, and Exodus 23:2, "One must incline after the
majority." So Rabbi Joshua wins the dispute. It is said that Rabbi Nathan
asked the Prophet Elijah, "What did the Holy One, blessed be He, do in that
hour?" He replied: "God smiled and said: 'My children have defeated Me,
my children have defeated Me.'"

wins although she is tired of him too, his sullen uncommunicativeness. She knows that the husband wants the son to win and is egging him along, in that solemn way. What she hates is that they must compete in the first place. Why must they, she thinks; damned genetic hardwiring, or is it damned society, social programming; that is the only puzzle.

Checkmate, thinks the son grimly, seeing his winning move. That's it, thinks the father, as scanning the board he sees the same move at the same moment, and straightens and sighs. He is cautious and gazes to the side of the son's right ear, his expression unchanging. The son continues looking at the board.

The mother is tired of them. The two of them. Damaged, smashed, crippled for life. If only she could intervene, thinks the angry grieving mother.

Where do you want to go for dinner, says the father. He sneaks a look out the window where it is still drizzling, and feels a healthy appetite coming on. A flock of pigeons, stitching downward across the window, pulls his glance all the way over to the son, whose eyes are still hidden, whose eyelids rest in a purple shadow. Good boy, he thinks, before he is able to stop himself, and feels his chest contract with a massive pleasure indistinguishable from suffering. So that the son finally raises his face to return the old man's gaze, so that the mother sees the smoothness of his brow, and her old husband's grooved forehead, in a single image, with the gray background of the rainy twilight. Wherever, says the triumphant son, looking directly now at the father's face. Wherever you think would be good.

The Sisters

Come out of their language. Try to go
back through the names they've given you.
I'll wait for you, I'm waiting for myself.
LUCE IRAGARAY

See-saw! See-saw!
We did it when we were kids,
A plank across a fallen log
And we'd fly,
Our braids would fly,
One up! One down!
Sister, it wasn't our plan
To fight over a man,
So why do we do it?
Why do they want us
To hate each other?
Babies! Make babies!
Make more than your enemy!
See-saw! Do it this way!
A demographic war

Is what you are good for,
And don't forget to weep
Later, when they are not,[†]
They say.
And we obey!

[†] "A voice was heard in Ramah, lamentation and bitter weeping; Rachel weeping for her children refused to be comforted for her children, because they were not," Jeremiah 31:15. Rachel is traditionally the mother of the exiled and slain children of Israel.

Rachel Solo

*And Laban went to shear his sheep; and Rachel
had stolen the images that were her father's. . . .
Now Rachel had taken the images, and put them
in the camel's furniture, and sat upon them.*
GENESIS 31: 20, 34

*What woman has not stolen? Who has not dropped
a few red herrings, mocked her way around the
separating bar, inscribed what made a difference
with her body . . . and with a transgression screwed
up whatever is successive?*
HELENE CIXOUS

Not getting mad, just getting even,
Papa, I'll say goodbye to you,
I'll load my camel with my goods
And take your household idols too,
And should you come in search of them
With indignation red and blue,
I'll sit upon your statuettes
And make good use of a bad taboo.
Papa, I'll say, *forgive me but
My monthly's here; don't misconstrue
This failure to get up.* . . . And you'll
Back off in dread. That's what you'll do.

The Interpretation of
Dreams

*And they said one to another, Behold, this dreamer
cometh. Come now therefore, and let us slay him,
and cast him into some pit, and we will say, Some
evil beast has devoured him; and we shall see what
will become of his dreams.*
GENESIS 37:19–20

*All dreams are dependent on the interpretation
given to them.*
MIDRASH RABBAH

*Take me, take me, I am coming down to you. Yes, all our
arms are outstretched, we almost have you, just a little
further. Come on, our brother. A trail of bubbles above me, I
pull myself hand over hand—weeds thicker than a father's
arms, rooted somewhere in the invisible silted floor, offer
themselves swaying. I gather strength and kick straight
downward. Am I there yet. Are you enclosing me. Yes, it is so
enjoyable here, heated, bowel-like, golden, shimmering,
green.*

*When you arrive and join us we will begin our journey, we
are all going to be rich, we are only waiting for you.*

❧

Our first fathers are alive in dream-time. There they are naked. There they are, naked. We can almost touch them. We ourselves can feel our identity with their bodies, which are their real selves. They are most fundamentally biological beings, family men, those who produce the next generation, the next link. They bless, but they have to beget before they can bless: their paternity is their deepest existence.

God creates. The patriarchs beget. (*Toledot*, begetting—cf. Gen 4:2, obliquely suggesting that God generates the cosmos through a sexual act.)

We can feel this. We remember their movements and gestures, their journeyings, the fine comedy of their family relations, living each other's lives, dying each other's deaths, as performances we ourselves have performed. Almost no separation yet. *I practically was or am all these men and women, who are or were me. The presence of El Shaddai, the Breasted One, the Mountain, brings them forward, enlarges them, making the borders between them, and between them and me, traversable, and preventing the intellectual distinction between life/dream, or myth/reality, or here/there, or conscious/sub-conscious, or yes/no from crystallizing. They fill up all the space, like the large, easy-breathing classical drawings of Picasso.*

Among the dream patriarchs nothing is yet repressed, everything is deep yet transparent, like a sea in motion, its tides and currents, and the way it rises up against the cliffs at its shoreline, reaches over boulders, rushes into caves, embraces the rock's least indentations. These patriarchs in their rising-up are always already falling and yet heaving forward again. Theirs are the ceaseless human rhythms, which we recognize as such only when we have already lost them.

With Joseph and his brothers, reality has imperceptibly changed. Without a break in the narrative, something has been broken. The sign of this is the "coat of many colors" to which a mysteriously romantic quality is attached. Why has this "coat of many colors" reiterated itself through a thousand puzzled interpretations yet remained a puzzle, like a bright square of embroidery appearing at a congress of international bankers? It is the dream-garment, materializing in consciousness at the very moment when "reality" and "dream" part company. Like all such signs it faces two ways. A sign of loss—parallel to the garments God makes for Adam and Eve, or the covering with which his two cautious sons cover the drunken Noah, or the hairy glove Jacob wears to defraud his father—yet at the same time a sign of love and a sign of luxury, "so light and delicate," say the rabbis, "it could be crushed and concealed in the closed palm of one hand." Rich colors for a spoiled son, his father's favorite.

We are approaching civilization as we know it. That is to say, recognizable family life as we know it. Joseph is the penultimate son born to a barren mother in the book of Genesis. God has removed (asuf) my reproach, says beautiful Rachel, and may God add (yosef) another son to me. Joseph is the darling, a pretty boy, "fair of form and fair to look at." Those same words having been used to describe Rachel. Joseph *is* Rachel, somehow, his father's pet: the rabbis say he painted his eyes and walked with mincing step. Showing off the coat of many colors, which old Jacob made him. Twirling, hugging himself. A young Hebrew Narcissus. No wonder his brothers hated him. No wonder they catch him in the field, strip him of his little coat and throw him into the pit, and sell him into Egypt, and rip the coat and dip it in goat's blood: exhibit A to show the father—do you recognize this coat, dad? A torn veil, a bloody show, a lost innocence.

Joseph dreams—what? Ten sheaves will bow down to one sheaf. The sun and moon and eleven stars also bow to him. He runs to tell the brothers; no wonder they want to get rid of him, the intolerable brat, the A student—nobody has a problem interpreting dreams like this. Later when Potiphar's wife tries to seduce him he is the exemplary servant of his master, purer than the pure, so that she is enraged and rips his garment off. Claims he tried to rape her, that familiar tale of the insulted woman who fails to understand the purity of the pretty young man. Another veil gone, another false deflowering.

Now Joseph the tease goes to prison. But he comes out again. Potiphar likes him and puts him in charge, the jailor likes him and puts him in charge. Pretty young man makes good, pleases the bosses, gets the job, God makes his hand prosper in all things and he is also unfailingly respectful to his superiors. . . . No doubt with all sincerity, unlike the tale of the rabbi who insisted on saying the sabbath prayer for the ruler with great ardor, explaining that one should always wish long life to the czar, since the next one was sure to be worse. . . .

Finally Pharaoh likes him very well and puts him in charge of the kingdom.

So the outsider/insider Joseph becomes prime minister, and

not for the last time. He obtains this position of power and influence despite his background, and over the protests of certain well-placed gentlemen who argue that if you let one of them in you'll be drowned in a sea of them before you turn around. An accurate assessment, as it eventuates; but the truth is that Joseph has efficiency and integrity in his favor. Nobody catches him with his hand in the till. Moreover, consider his impressive capacity for assimilation: he has excellent manners, dresses well if a bit austerely, marries his old employer's daughter (Potiphar's daughter! so much for Potiphar's wife, that old she-bear). You would never take him for one of . . . well, you know what I'm talking about . . . if it were not for the slight accent, which many of the ladies in any case consider superlatively charming. Above all is his brilliance in an area people really care about. Dreams. What does my dream mean? What does my life mean? What will happen next? Oh, you'll be promoted. Oh, you'll be hung. Oh, your kingdom will have seven fat years followed by seven years of famine so it would be a good idea for you to put someone competent in charge of the granaries. Who do you suppose that should be. No, don't thank me, thank the Holy One who lets me know these things, explains Joseph modestly.

Finally the day arrives for which we have all been waiting. Joseph's brothers come down to Egypt during the famine. They are here to buy grain. Everyone at home is on the verge of starvation. The officials send them with all the other petitioners to make their request of the prime minister, sitting draped in his magisterial robes. Do they recognize this prime minister? No. Does he recognize them? What do you think. Does he tease them? What do you think. Torment them? What do you think. Heap grain on them, feast them, refuse to take their money, accuse them of theft, refuse to release them unless they bring their youngest brother Benjamin to court—while the old father at home laments that if he loses Benjamin, Rachel's only other son, it will bring down his gray hairs with sorrow to the grave— and when Joseph sees the boy Benjamin does he hide himself in an antechamber to weep? What do you think. In the end he reveals himself, joyously restoring the family unity. And morally as well as materially generous? The brothers are feeling guilty, and understandably anxious about Joseph's possible future behavior. So Joseph reassures them: you thought you were doing me harm, but you see it was all God's plan. By this time the family is greatly expanded, so full of begats that "all the souls that came out of the loins of Jacob were seventy souls," not to mention wives and servants, all of whom will now live happily ever after.

I have a family, you have a family. Some of our brothers are princes, some not so princely. And the children? They're well, they're in good health, they graduated college already, they're getting married? To have children is a blessing, sometimes not such a blessing. God willing, we should all be so lucky as Jacob, such a good son he had, such a smart boychik.

Nonetheless the coat of many colors materializes at the moment of loss. A symbol of something else. A symbol of *symbolism*. The material object evoking the maternal subject: matter for pride and arrogance on the part of the naively exhibitionist child, matter for the mutter on the part of his jealous brothers, patchwork of Israel's sensuous love for Rachel-Joseph, fabric for another kind of story, a new velvet moment.

Goodbye, goodbye to the family; when one adaptable brother can leave the backwoods—but we do not know they are the backwoods until he leaves, we thought "home" was the world—for the big city, where he will become rich and powerful. Where his family will become his pathetic dependents and he their magnanimous protector. Does the mysterious bond of the family fail? No, but we see now that it might fail, it is susceptible to failure, the advent of the individual such as Joseph destroys the powerful biological balance of the mythic family. In the successions of brothers Cain and Abel are bonded forever, Abraham and Lot are balanced, Isaac and Ishmael are balanced, Jacob and Esau are balanced—although one in each pair is the chosen link in God's chain, the kinsmen remain inhabitants of a shared world. But in the generation of Joseph and his brothers the filial bond becomes a matter of human choice. The brothers choose to reject it. Joseph chooses to restore it.

Feel free to use my limousine, boys. I'll send my tailor over in the morning. Charge it on my card, listen, here's the key to the liquor cabinet. Just don't worry about a thing, you'll be looked after, your children also. What can be more precious to a man than his family.

He unbends, he chokes back the tears, he embraces them. At the moment of intimacy he weeps unreservedly. It is said that to reveal himself to his brothers he shows his circumcised penis. It is said that he speaks Hebrew to them. Yet it is also said that at this moment Judah releases a scream that causes the walls to shake and Pharaoh to fall off his throne.

🖾

The biological family belongs to dream-time and myth-space.

The brothers, acting on personal resentment, break the magic circle. Joseph is ejected out of dream-time into the practical world of a complex society. A class structure. A wealthy household, keeping the books and overseeing the estate, sexual novelty surrounding him (which he rejects, but it must be educational), jail, the pharaonic court, political maneuvering, imperial economic policy. Clean as a whistle, pure as a lily, smelling like a desert rose, Joseph rises like a cork—from foreign slave to headman in three easy lessons. Nothing succeeds like success. But the secret of his success is that Joseph brings with him a piece of dream-time. Which is the world of biological life, the processes of nature, and the purposes of God. To interpret a dream is to read a sequence of hieroglyphs in the book of nature. Sheaves of wheat. Sun moon stars. Branches of ripe grapes. Baskets of bread and birds to peck at them. Fat and lean kine. Healthy and thin ears of corn. The rabbis say that Joseph could interpret Pharaoh's dream because he dreamed the same dream, at the same moment as Pharaoh. And does not interpretation belong to God? asks Joseph.

One follows the clues by allowing them to announce themselves. Yet from the beginning there is only one story. Down there, down there. Under the surface where it is green, where it is gold. Of course there is only one story, flung forth in projection, displacement, compression, repression. The papa-mama story, can I come in for a snuggle, at the center of the labyrinth a minor taurus, she did it, that one, with a bull. With a will. Certain words in all languages mean themselves and their opposites simultaneously. These are ur-words, pointing us to the dream-language. In the dream-realm we find no negative or contradiction. In this respect it springs from the realm of nature, place of censorless ceaseless becoming.

Dream, saga, folk tale, myth. The individual-collective imagination at its bright labors. He, the hero, leaves home crosses
river meets sorcerer meets witch slays dragon captures princess: if he goes all the way, he goes all the way home—Papa,
it's me! Dream and myth, children holding hands, living each
other's lives, dying each other's deaths. A bony animal means
suffering. The sun signifies wealth. Beware the drowned man.
The truth, the lie.

The power of the dream is the power of the biological family.
The papa-mama story. So the power of the family is intact
during the life of Joseph. But already the fabric is thin, the coat
of many colors has been ripped to shreds, the family hangs by a
thread, the tenuous fiber of personal longing that God has
created in a world of nations and national policy. Egypt,
Babylonia, Persia, their palaces, their treasures, their idle royal
families, priesthoods, dusty bureaucracies are the stuff of reality. God has created this copious world—the nations, the empires—as well, but the nations do not know it yet. Soon,
therefore, we must transcend the dream-life, the family-life.
We too must become a nation.

What might fail must fail. That is story logic. Just as with the
apple, if it might be eaten it must be eaten.

We know this loss already, a pathos far in our past. Every detail
of the story confirms it. When Joseph weeps because of the
restoration of the family, and the brothers weep with relief that
he is not about to punish them, and when Joseph falls on his
father's neck and weeps a good while, and when Jacob on his
deathbed strengthens himself to sit up—I had not thought to
have seen thy face, and lo, God hath shown me also thy seed, he

says triumphantly to Joseph—we know the dream-family is gone, aye ages long ago. The world as we know it is men sitting in business suits and silk ties in committee rooms.

Yet it is said that Torah puts on the garments of this world. It is said that the essence of the garment is the body, the essence of the body is the soul, it is said that all is connected, this one to that one—the coat of many colors, sign of a lost dream, strangely fails to fade. Nothing is lost, they say. Look at the colors, they remain sumptuous as ever. Look at it heal itself and become whole. Dream, say the rabbis of Joseph, is one level; vision is one level; prophecy is one level. All are levels within levels, one above the other. It is said that the above is like the below. Is it true? Is it true? *Take me, take me, I am coming down to you. Yes, all our arms are outstretched, we almost have you.*

Legend into History
The Fathers II

The Nursing Father

*And the Angel of the Lord appeared
unto him in a flame of fire out of the
midst of a bush: and he looked, and,
behold, the bush burned with fire, and
the bush was not consumed.*
EXODUS 3:2

This story made it possible to tell other stories.
MICHAEL WALZER, *EXODUS AND REVOLUTION*

What was Egypt, that God sent us down into it and with an outstretched arm brought us up out of it. A flat plane extended on either side of a great river. A place without mountains. The reifying of the abstract body. The elegance of the linear, particularly the sides and slender waists, slender and static in all the representations, the flat torsos elongated along a plane whether of stone or swamp-papyrus, in stasis without stiffness, sheerly vitally vibrant those waists, the shoulders with their slender arms, the delicate refinement of body. They were dancers in delirium, those sisters, those slaves, their animals as well, the Ibis and the Ram, the exquisite thinness of their fabrics like the refinement of their ankles. No fatness. No excess. Among their gods and goddesses reigned a pure ancient graciousness, neither excessively angular nor excessively curvilinear, but refined over many centuries into perfection and beyond perfection into trance. To entrance. The entrance to timelessness.

For in that aeons-long expanse of Egypt we discern the swollen desire of timelessness. There must nothing happen. The river floods, recedes. There are wars. There are revolutions. It is nothing. Dynasties—nothing. The same sun-Amen, the same river, the double of the cool river underground, the same slaves or almost the same, the same scribes writing the same annals, the same priests whispering the same intrigues, the same slender body of the goddess Nut arched as if in permanent sexual pleasure from the eastern to the western limit of the world, tinted a heavenly shade of blue in which gleaming spots of golden stars are strewn, the same Isis and Osiris, the same Horus and Set, the same death and dismemberment, the same renewal and recovery. There is nothing happening and nothing to happen, it is all old. All is known. There is no growth or decay. There is no death, there cannot be, the spirit glides in her slender boat out along the dark river, jeweled and scented, arrayed and sandaled, surrounded by her playthings, and she replies to the gatekeeper Osiris, and is weighed against a feather, and passes beyond. The body, packed in resin, may wait and wait. Sealed absolutely from the air.

Upon papyrus, upon stone, upon gold, this perfect flatness or this perfectly accurate lineation. The volumes of sculpture the same. The expressionless representations bring forth in the viewer however an exquisite awareness of one's back and shoulders, androgynous sides and waist, one's most sinuous catlike self. However miniature or colossal the form, including the seated emperor and empress side by side on their double throne, including the guardian deities at Luxor or Memphis, including the crouched indifferent sphinx, and the deaf pyramids, it is all luxury, calm, voluptuousness, a motionless final dance.

It is upon the bodies of their slaves that they dance.

But above all the Eye. The Egyptian Eye. In the form of a smooth fruit with its stem; its lid extended, painted iridescent blue, thick kohl for the lashes. The extracted, abstracted Egyptian Eye.

It is an invitation. It is a spy, perhaps a court spy. You do not watch this Eye but you are watched. The Eye does not close, the Eye will not blink. The Eye regards everything but imagines nothing. It lies in the palm of the hand. It is a hieroglyph inscribed on a wall. Not a voice, it emits no sound. Merely its identical self like other hieroglyphs, an image, it has no further significance. It signifies, precisely, nothing beyond what it is, physically, that is the ubiquitous Egyptian Eye. It is the Evil Eye. A male eye, a female?

On the pulp of their slaves the refined Egyptians dance. Not the house slaves and palace slaves, who are taught to resemble their masters and mistresses. These have the most refined manners, graceful and even scented bodies. But outside. Oh—somewhere outside. Those whose bodies are disturbingly muscled, organisms to perform work. The subhuman. Those who, when they die, do not revive but simply rot.

📛

 A hiatus: I disappear into Egypt, or seem to, for four hundred years. I am enslaved there. It is my first captivity. I am a hot foreign body of herdsmen—nomadic and

semi-nomadic, restless, sometime hunters, sometime primitive farmers, sometime mercenaries, sometime thieves, living by nature under no law, possessing military combined with pastoral virtues. I am their stranger. I am their Other, to them an abomination. Like the God of my fathers I need to travel in order to breathe, but am trapped like a scarab in amber. Egypt is the not-me, the not-us, highly feminized but alien, a reverie of no-change, no-motion, no-wilderness, no-death, no-birth.

◲

A child is born. Bursts from the amber: imago, energy, genius. Tell us the story! Tell us the story! A story! Well, to begin— even before his conception, then at his birth and in his infancy, the story is all women. You remember the two midwives who refuse to kill the male Hebrew babies? A non-confrontational civil disobedience, they report that the Hebrew mothers are so lively they give birth before the midwives arrive. Then, you remember the mother of Moses? She doesn't kill him either, she hides him and then she packs him (a live baby!) into a little floating basket and sets it among the reeds of the riverbank (bright green river of life, not black river of death!) where a beautiful princess who wants a baby finds him. And you know what they say? When the princess unwrapped Moses he cried so loud she knew he had to be a Jew. Naturally she decides to keep him (women are disloyal to civilization; women want babies) and then Moses' own sister who has been hiding in the reeds pops out and asks Pharaoh's daughter: would you like me to find you a nurse for that nice baby? The princess says yes, so Miriam runs fast and fetches Moses' own mother who then gets to breast-feed Moses for three years. Isn't that clever? Do you like the way all the brave women combine in the resistance? Do you notice how they collaborate across racial and class lines, defying the law of empire to save a child's life?[†] Of course it is also possible that the baby is really the illegitimate child of the princess. Some men consider this the most important point in the story.[‡] But the essence of the story is the birth, and protected rearing in a palace, of the rebellious child.

Child of compassion, child of wrath. Moses is Egyptian, he is Hebrew, he is both/neither, he is insider/outsider, he is compressed/torn. Child of the mothers in the world of the fathers. He is the locus of gain/loss, he is where another division begins. Between the God of the universe and the God of a tribe, between inclusion and exclusion, between the imperative of liberty and the imperative of law, explodes Moses. What we know about him is exactly nothing, exactly everything, he is a fierce mystery.

[†] In addition to the collaboration of Pharaoh's daughter, scholars are uncertain whether the midwives, whose names (Shifrah and Puah) are not Hebrew, are Egyptians or Israelites.

[‡] Perhaps nobody has ever heard the tale of Moses' "adoption" by the daughter of pharaoh without thinking the same thing. Freud, in *Moses and Monotheism*, however, insists that Moses could not have been a Hebrew since this tribe was too primitive to have invented monotheism; therefore Moses must have been an Egyptian devotee of the cult of Akhneton. The logic is unclear: why must the future leader be biologically Egyptian to be the carrier of an Egyptian ideological strain? We are perhaps seeing a bit of anti-Semitism here, Freud perhaps thinks the Jews were too inferior racially to have produced a Moses. This seems only slightly more foolish than thinking that Shakespeare came from too base a social class to have written Shakespeare's plays. But Freud too was both insider/outsider, a European, a Jew, a problem in the history of assimilation.

But the story? Stepping outside the palace for the first time in his life, like the adolescent Buddha (remember that "story" equals "life" according to our purposes) the young Moses encounters political reality. He sees an Egyptian foreman beat a Hebrew slave; he glances both ways, nobody is watching, he kills the foreman. Next day he sees two Hebrews fighting and chides the aggressor, who responds belligerently: Who made you our judge? Will you kill me too, the way you killed the Egyptian? So Moses is afraid; he flees the city. Like the Buddha (seven centuries away) whose eyes were opened with horror at disease, old age, and death. No, unlike the Buddha. Unlike, unlike. This anger of Moses that flares spontaneously. This hatred of slavery. This question of social justice.

What does the Buddha care for social justice? The Buddha counsels us to escape this world of suffering, from which Moses won't escape, from which he escapes to return, bearing twice his weight, bearing his infinite burden, bearing the weight of God. And the weight of the Hebrew people as well—infinitely, impossibly heavy. Already his destiny is shaped: to hate slavery, to hate violence, to be violent and enslaved—forever—to the God of the Fathers. And never to be loved or understood. Who made you judge; will you kill us the way you killed the Egyptian? They mock him ungratefully, servilely—and they will continue to do so. Why can't we have our fleshpots, they will whine, why can't we eat fish the way we did in Egypt, instead of this boring manna, why can't we have our cucumbers melons leeks onions garlic, why can't we dance around a golden calf, how do you expect us to fight Canaanites, they're bigger than we are.

Never to be loved, remember that. To bear this ungrateful

people, this stupid servile people, this people without memory, this disobedient people, like a monstrous child at his breast, a mindless, colicky, sickly child—to save it alive but not to be loved by it. To plead with God for its ungrateful life, to carry it to freedom, to build it finally into a nation and tell it what is required of it—again and again the story of emancipation. To create a memory for it. To create law for it. To create purpose. To force it into history. But never to be loved, and then to die in the sight of the Land but not to enter it.

For God is going to use him. God doesn't care whether he is a Hebrew or an Egyptian, or some interesting combination, only that he is a powerful pack animal. Of all those who were called by God and resisted the calling, Moses is most tragic—not because God abandons him but on the contrary because God seizes on him and employs him ruthlessly, to the outer limits of his extraordinary endurance. God will press him. God will squeeze him like an orange, extracting juice and pulp, and throw him away like peel. With Moses God plays no games. No hiding-and-showing. After the four hundred year absence, not a word of greeting. From the day he sees the burning bush until the day of his death forty years afterward, Moses will move through life bearing the two weights. The weight of God from above, crushing him. The weight of the Israelites at his bosom, a hateful infant refusing the nipple. Because God is ready now to rupture the ancient Near Eastern timelessness.

(If God wishes to push through heaven's membrane, from being beyond time to being within time, if God wants himself to move in the arrowlike temporal dimension, away from being Elohim, Transcendent Heavenly Being(s), or El Shaddai, Almighty God of the Breast-Hill-Mountain, or El Olam, Everlasting, if God chooses to cruise the unknown, if God desires to be named I WILL BECOME THAT I WILL BECOME,[†] then a nation is required to receive his covenant. To embody his undeclared purposes. If a nation, then a leader. If a leader, then cruelty; which in any case people understand. But also a promise.)

🖾

I write in American space and Jewish time. The space of my particular promised land. Sweet land of liberty.
Land to which my grandfathers fled, with their socialist pamphlets. With their eyes of two thousand years sorrow. With their backs of the tired, the poor, the huddled masses yearning to breathe free. With Galician and Lithuanian villages burning behind them. In the village squares—it was nothing new—they were lining up the Jews. Pamphlets were being distributed declaring that Jews in obscene rituals killed Christian babies, the newspapers printed cartoons of evil men with liverish lips and hook noses squatting on cities. The icon of a bulging moneybag signified a Jew. In the village squares stood blond soldiers who would take an old man by the earlock, hold a revolver to his neck, command him to spit on his Torah. My grandfathers with their fantasy, as it so happens, about universal brotherhood, withheld their hands from retaliation.

How do I know I am a Jew in Jewish time. I am in Budapest twenty years ago, a fine restaurant, as I am leaving the

---

[†] God's name Eyheh asher eyheh, usually translated in English "I am that I am," is ambivalent as to verb tense; Eyheh in each case may be "I am" or "I will be." Commentators have proposed numerous translations and meanings; Buber and others see the name as conveying a kind of future perfect sense.

*maitre d' engages me in conversation for some reason, it is
small talk, nothing. And you are American; yes, American.
And your people . . . ? My people, my grandparents came over
all in the eighteen eighties from eastern Europe. Yes, he says,
with his eyes of two thousand years which I have not noticed.
We call them the glückische kinder.*

The lucky children.

When he saw the burning bush he was fascinated. He walked
closer. The thornbush, grown out of a rock cleft in the shrubby
Midian hills, was aflame but not "burning" in the sense that it
was not eaten. It was enduring, or perhaps regenerating itself
moment by moment while fire bit at it and hissed around it.
Inside the fire whirled twenty-two letters, like imps. He did not
know that the bush, from which the Presence spoke and commanded, was an image of himself. He was regarding his own
future, seething red and blue—on holy ground—where the
Presence was God, was a demon, was everything.[†] This power
would use the good of Moses, his evil, his everything. Would
not leave his intelligence, his imagination, his courage, his
conscience, his power to persuade, his power to command—
would not leave his energies alone ever again. Nor scrupled to
employ his fanaticism, his pride, his aristocratic Egyptian haugh-
tiness, his impatience, his violence, his cold abstractedness—

[†] Buber in *I and Thou* writes: "Man receives . . . a Presence, a Presence as
power . . . it makes life heavier, insupportably heavy, but heavy with meaning. Meaning now is assured. Nothing henceforth can any longer be mean-
ingless."

every quality a kindly man might hate in himself, the God of
History used those too.

Like others called by God, Moses resisted. *Hineni,* here am I, in
the first instance. But soon: Why me, I'm only a stutterer, I'm
not capable. What do you want from me and why must it be so
difficult. A wise instinct, because the God of History will lead
him a little at a time as if he were a pet dog. Or a work dog. Not
the shepherd but the shepherd's dog. Yapping at the flock's
heels.

Moses discovers the will of God in the bush. Here am I. In the
bush, and again in the voice, and again in the night attack from
which Zipporah saves him. A bloody husband you are to me,
cries the Hittite wife to the Hebrew husband, casting a foreskin
at his feet. Then again in the writhing snake that immobilizes to
a rod. And again in the plagues, and again in the Red Sea
(Moses carrying the bones of Joseph), when a strong east wind
all night made the sea go back, and the waters were divided so
that people passed through a corridor with waves like topless
gelatinous walls on their right hand and their left, and could see
fish and other creatures and plants of the deep captured swimming inside, and again when the Red Sea overwhelmed the
pursuing armies, finally drowning their horses, horsemen and
chariots, and Miriam led the women in a victory dance praising
God with drums and timbrels, and again in manna (unlike the
fleshpots in Egypt), and again marching behind the ghostly
pillar of fire and pillar of smoke (unlike the stick figure deities
in Egypt), and again in thunder and fierce lightning and quak-
ing and the sound of the trumpet in Sinai that they say is a ram's
horn, the same ram Abraham slew on Moriah. Onward. Get on
with it. And again in the Law; and again in the destruction of

the golden calf; and again in the defeat of Amalek; and again inside the quiet wooden tabernacle which is like the ark in which his infant body was placed to float among the reeds, which is like Jochabed's uterus, the twin seraphim carved facing one another as labia, where God speaks to Moses face to face as a man speaks with a friend. Bliss then. Onward. Again when Moses begs that the Presence accompany the Israelites forever, separating them from other peoples, and the Presence agrees. God says to Moses: I'm here. I'm not gone. I'm always here. Tenderly. Ominously.

And again when God's anger is kindled and breaks out and destroys those who complain; and makes seventy elders prophecy; and strikes Miriam with leprosy for her claim that he speaks to her; and swears by his life that none who left Egypt will enter Canaan because they are all slaves in their hearts except Joshua, so let their carcasses rot in the wilderness. Let only the young and free possess the Land. Get on with it. Any of these signs would have been sufficient. And again when he makes the earth swallow Korah and his men alive into the pit for rebellion; and again when Aaron's rod blooms simultaneously with buds, blossoms and almonds; and when twenty-four thousand die of plague after following Moabite gods; and again when he (Moses) is able before death to state the entire Torah to the Israelites, and to sing that we suck honey from the rock; and again when he is commanded to climb Mount Pisgah, and survey the whole of the holy land from Sinai to Galilee, and then to die.

Any of these signs would have been sufficient.

And the purpose of the story? From a despicable mob to create a free, disciplined, self-governing nation. With a rule of law composed by God instead of a king. A nation without a king. With stress on social justice; commandments of generosity to the poor; periodic release of debts and slaves; periodic release of the land, which it is understood belongs to God, not to human beings, so that all "private property" is temporary. A commandment not to afflict widows and orphans in any way, because if they cry at all to God he will surely hear their cry, and his wrath will wax hot, and he will kill you with the sword, and your wives will be widows and your children fatherless. A commandment to love God (love! with all your heart, mind and strength) and your neighbor as yourself, for the Lord makes this covenant with the whole people, not merely its rulers, for the whole people under this covenant will be a nation sacred to God. Repeated reminders that the law applies equally to rich and poor, to native and stranger. Repeated, repeated injunctions against oppressing the stranger, because you know the heart of the stranger, because you were strangers in Egypt.

All of which appears impossible, since the people are constantly backsliding and seem unable to remember from one day to the next even a simple thing like God's getting them through the Red Sea, much less a complicated set of laws. The fact is, nobody likes this project of liberty very much.

◼

Egypt, Succoth, Sea of Reeds, Marah the Bitter, Horeb, Sinai, Moab, Gilead, Pisgah, Canaan. *Babylon, Rome, Ethiopia, India, Persia, Spain, Portugal, the Low Countries, Germany, Poland, Russia, England, France, America.* Auschwitz, Bergen Belson, Buchenwald, Theresienstadt, Dachau, Treblinka,

Chelmno, Sobibor, Belzik, Maidanek. *Montgomery, Little Rock, Greensboro, Nashville, Atlanta, Albany, Birmingham, Washington, D.C., Jackson, Meridian, Harlem, Chicago, Watts, Selma, Memphis.* Wilderness.

🗝

Oh freedom. Oh freedom. Oh freedom over me.
And before I'll be a slave I'll be buried in my grave
And go home to my Lord and be free.

A song learned at the same time as I learned the others. Go down Moses. We shall not, we shall not be moved. The task of mending the earth. Incredible folly even to let the words take form between one's ears—when did I assume such a burden? Where did I sign on God's dotted line? With my mother's milk. With invisible ink. When Moses killed the Egyptian, when I watched two pimpled white girls in the bathroom pull a small black girl's braids and push their faces up to her and laugh showing their teeth as if they were going to bite her, when the Russian soldier said filthy Jew to my great grandmother, when my father came home from his Union meetings, and at a hundred thousand other moments. When I went to Pioneer Youth Camp where we did Long may our land be bright, With freedom's holy light, and No More Auction Block for Me. Where we sang Tzena Tzena, and danced the hora in the barn.

At the campfires the girls and boys sat in separate whispering clumps, except for those who were already boyfriend-and-girlfriend. We passed forbidden candy. The boys would shove one of their number at a group of us, shouting, and we shoved him back even if we wanted him. The counsellors would move around the fire swiftly, featureless shadows, throwing more wood on or adjusting logs at the edges. I wondered how they could dare to go close to it, this fire that to me seemed so great and hot, hurling huge flickering reddish lights among us while we sat with moist dirt and grass under our blankets. Our faces would be roasted although we were shivering.

What we did in the dark was sing. I loved the sound of our voices together. Oppressed so hard they could not stand was like when the kids in my building at home ganged up on me. Get her. Grabbed my book, tossed it in the mud, taunted Who do you think you are, Einstein? I am only a junior pioneer but already I know about the world we are working for, the no more hatred and persecution, the no more war, no more cruel oppression. One world. The end of ignorance and prejudice. I know the words of the songs and can harmonize the way my father showed me. Around the flames all the campers swayed from side to side with our arms around each other's small bodies. If I had a Hammer . . . I'd hammer out love between my brothers and my sisters, Aaall over this land. We look at the red sparks flying from the top of the fire.

After the campfire we have to find our way through the woods to our cabins. I wandered off the narrow dirt trail, banged against standing trees and dead ones, scratched by invisible branches. Fell in a sea of dry leaves. Starting to crawl instead of walk. Starting to cry, hearing the unbroken mockery of crickets, the voices of the older campers still singing.

Nobody understands this project of liberty, it is far too difficult. They do, however, understand terror. Whoever is on my side (God's side) go out into the camp and every man slay his brother, his son, his friend and neighbor. They do understand fanatic intolerance. No other Gods. No images, no idols, no interbreeding, no whoring with the Others, whom the God of History has not chosen. What if the Others are great and we are little? Still they are the unclean, the not-us. Division of clean from unclean. Pure from defiled. Righteous from unrighteous. The universality of God—this monotheism which is now digging its massive root down to the core of the planet—leads along one branch to universal love and compassion, an infinite cherishing of life, a new ethics: They shall not hurt nor destroy in all my holy mountain. Along another branch it becomes the laws of science. Gravity, motion, chemistry, everywhere reasonable, everywhere consistent: This selfsame logic, says Johannes Kepler, the creator placed in our minds so that we might share in his ideas. Along yet another branch, Sinai feeds the tenacious pride of those who consider themselves chosen, who will rejoice at the death of the unbeliever, the death of the apostate. It is a pride that will precipitate oppression, suffering, and martyrdom, the spilled blood of century after century, in religion after religion. It is a pride that will encourage the narrowness of the narrow in spirit, let there be no mistake. And as for the flower of intellectual evil that has most gorgeously blossomed in our own century, the doctrine of racial purity: this too, with its rhetoric, its simple appeal, is rooted in Sinai. For what is a Master Race if not the distorted mirror image of a Chosen People, at which all the devils in Gehenna laugh until their sides split?

But as for Moses, our pack animal, destruction of the wayward is not his desire. When they worship the golden calf Moses prevents God from destroying all the Israelites—the Egyptians will laugh at you and think you're crazy—remember what you promised Abraham Isaac and Jacob, shouts Moses at the Almighty; then he goes down the mountain and orders the massacre in which three thousand men are slaughtered; then desperately climbs Sinai again and demands: forgive them! And if you will not—then blot my name from your book! And when they all weep for meat instead of manna, Moses turns on God: why do you lay this burden on me? Did I beget this people? Did I give birth to them, that you require me to carry them like a nursing father on my bosom, to the land you promised their fathers? Where am I to get meat for them? From my own body? Kill me then! They are too heavy for me to bear.

ᔕ

And all the while the Eye of Egypt is being defeated. Instead of Image we possess Word. An alternative beauty bursts into existence, through the tongue of the stutterer Moses. It is the triumph of the Ear, vision sublimated into language. Nothing remains to see—God is perfectly invisible, impalpable—only to hear. Listen! The Lord thy God, the Lord is One, says Moses. One gives us the Law. Therefore the Law and the Prophets, the Law and its interpretations, all oral tradition, all written commentaries, all words regarding the Word shall become portions of Torah, twigs on a tree of life, rooted in Sinai, exfoliating in time and space until the end of the world.

Gives us a Book, gives us therefore the life of the mind, gives us the intellectual power to survive in exile—and if in that act is a perpetual bondage, there is also a perpetual liberation from bondage: for are we not commanded by the text itself to interrogate, to engage in dialogue with each other, with the text, with God? Turn it and turn it, says Talmud, for everything is in it. Talmud says: there is always another interpretation. Talmud says: each question that a pupil will ever pose to a teacher, Moses already heard at Sinai. Words unlike images are indestructible. Words unlike images are powerful yet indeterminate, slip and slide (it's their strength, they wrestle, look at the shining sweat on them) and escape when you think you have them pinned, contain immeasurable dark interiors.

The image is motionless, timeless. It gives itself to you immediately. But language moves, it exists only in time, in history, the past melting and rushing toward the future, provoking you, dancing away. Infinitely heavy, infinitely plural, ungraspable—like God—a perpetual guarantee against slavery.

But remember the women. What do the women say?

The women say that the triumph of the Word presupposes and produces the repression of the Mother. Again and further. Sensuous perception is subordinated to intellectual principle. The invisibility of God implies the paternity of God. For the Father is that-which-must-be deduced, while the Mother remains evident to the senses.[†] And so it seems that the goddess is finally

---

[†] The dematerialized, imageless God who "was to have neither a name nor a countenance" is for Freud "a triumph of spirituality over the senses" and a chief reason for the endurance of Judaism despite persecution. A second reason for the endurance of Judaism according to Freud is that the religion contains a repressed memory of the assassination of Moses by his rebellious people. From another point of view it looks as if it is Freud who needs to kill the spiritual father and to project the deed upon his ancestors. Yet the theory of a textual unconscious is strengthened when we propose that it was not Moses who was killed at the advent of monotheism, but the rival gods, especially the mother goddess, and that the (imperfectly) repressed memory of that murder is among the most profound sources of energy within Judaism.

deposed. She whose religion flourished for thousands of years before his advent; who was creatrix of earth and supplier of agriculture; who invented law, protected women in childbirth, created writing, led armies, entered into union with her young beloved, regulated the ablutions of her priestesses and ascended and descended with the moon.

Elsewhere when one people conquers another the number of gods increases. The new ones join the old, some are promoted and some demoted. Witness Hinduism, the textbook case of syncretism in which augmentation is the rule, nothing is lost, and dozens of divinities coexist in layers of various provenance as if no deity once alive can ever die. With the God of Moses it is different. When this one descends on Canaan, the rest must disappear; we must all agree that they never existed.

But what if a god once alive can never die?

They are denied, that is to say they are eaten. Devoured, swallowed, absorbed, their bundles of attributes digested. They wait. And sometimes one feels them kick.

"Come not near your wives," commands God to Israel before Sinai—and so we suddenly learn that women are perhaps not included in the Covenant?[†] Yes, it is in the life of Moses that we see the women disappear. We see the flash of their backs as they

---

[†] "At the central moment of Jewish history, women are invisible . . . how is it . . . that the text could imply we were not there?" asks Judith Plaskow in *Standing Again at Sinai*. Deuteronomy 29: 10–11 attempts to correct for the slippage, asserting the presence of the entire congregation: "Ye stand this day all of you before the Lord your God; your captains of your tribes, your elders, and your officers, with all the men of Israel, your little ones, your wives, and the stranger that is in thy camp, from the hewer of thy wood to

dive, like dolphins, beneath the agitated surface of the text.
Where are they now, bold midwives, mothers, sisters, disobedient princesses, bitter talking-back wives. Submerged; objects of
the law; apparently passive. You shall not suffer a witch to live.
A daughter is her father's possession. He may sell her if he
wishes. A woman's husband is her lord, she cannot initiate
divorce, she cannot inherit property except where there is no
male heir. The punishment if a bride is not a virgin, or a woman
is convicted of adultery, is death by stoning. The woman, the
mother, the cycle of maternity, is now said to be intrinsically
unclean. Her menstrual blood defiles. Her secretions are the
paradigm for every kind of pustulance or running sore, diseases
requiring isolation and ritual cleansing. Leprosy is figuratively
a female disease: the reason Miriam but not Aaron is punished
by it. Before and after menstruation a woman is unclean. She is
also unclean after childbirth, and longer if the child is a girl. If
she touches you during these periods you become defiled. If
you touch her bed, or something she has sat on, you are defiled.[†]

Yet do prohibitions not draw one's (secret) attention to that
which is prohibited? Do these prohibitions not make the defil-
ing thing at once disgusting and attractive? Not even to *touch*

---

the drawer of thy water." The midrash adds that God at Sinai remembered
his error of speaking only to Adam about the tree of knowledge and decided
that women would nullify the Torah if they were not spoken to first.

[†] Judy Grahn argues in *Blood, Bread and Roses* that menstrual rites including the isolation of the menstruant, timed with the moon, were originally
invented by women and represent human societies' earliest recognition of
cosmic order and our relation to it. If this is the case, the regulation of
menstruant women within systems of male law parallels the appropriation of
procreativity by the male God. Julia Kristeva argues in *Powers of Horror* that
Biblical uncleanness in general is semiotically female, representing the dread
of the maternal. Mary Douglas in *Purity and Danger* proposes that a society's

the place where a menstruating woman, or a woman after child-birth, has sat. One almost wishes her to sit, to have sat, every-where. One can almost smell it. The fetishism of the nose, like any fetishism, strongest when the object is present only to the imagination. So the reduction of the woman's power, the eleva-tion of the abstract father whom one cannot see, contribute to the power of the covenant? The woman pollutes? Very well: exorcise her, isolate her, erase her (she will rule your dreams).

Listen. In the time of the Temple, the sacrifice of animals, extremely voluptuous and requiring that blood be splashed everywhere (yes, on the men), is a displaced sacrifice of the woman whom you cannot afford to sacrifice in person. Previ-ously it was her firstborn child, who opened the matrix of her womb, which you sacrificed instead of the mother. Now you sacrifice the animal as substitute for both child and mother. And you throw the blood all over the building and the people. And the blood stinks like a woman.

The subduing of the Eye (the evil Egyptian Eye) is complete. Instead of a graven image, God is language. But the subduing of the body, the subduing of woman? Apparently defeated yet far from defeat, she invisibly propagates, increases and multi-plies throughout the laws, statutes, and ordinances designed to contain her. Because no substitute exists for her sexual vitality,

---

ideas of purity and impurity express by analogy that society's larger order-ing principles. "Defilement is never an isolated event. It cannot occur except in view of a systematic ordering of ideas." What constitutes "abomination" in Leviticus, she argues, is anything that suggests blurring, ambiguity, or nonconformity to category; hybrids and mixings are "unclean." What is holy is like God: "one, pure, complete." Here again then we see the theme of division, reified as sacred order.

her practical capacity, here in the world of generation which God has made according to his Will. (Where is the promised land? If it were beyond the flesh it would be Egypt.) And if *ruach*, spirit, is a woman; if *hokhmah*, wisdom, is a woman; if *rachmanes*, God's attribute of compassion, derives from the mother's womb; if the sabbath is a bride; if the *shekhinah* is daughter, bride, mother, moon, sea, faith, wisdom, and speech; and if *Torah* herself is the king's child who shows herself little by little to her lovers—then it is *inside the language*, the place of interpretation, the place of dialogue, interrogation, commentary, laughter, the place of holy disobedience, the site of persistent stubbornness, wrestling, and the demand for blessing, foreseen from the rim of eternity by the Holy One who has curiously chosen this rebellious people for his especial treasure—here in the place of metaphor is where she waits.

And therefore the rabbis say the Shekhinah, who is the feminine portion of God, became the spouse of Moses, replacing Zipporah. They claim that the Shekhinah accompanied him always and filled him with secret joy. And telling of his death, they say that on Mount Pisgah Moses refuses to die. God sends the Angel of Death for him but Moses thrice rejects the summons. Finally God says he will permit Moses to live on condition that Israel dies. Only then does Moses surrender to God and consent to die; and the Shekhinah bends down and kisses him on the lips. On this kiss his spirit travels to heaven.

🏵

 Leaving me behind to possess the land and lose it, possess it and lose it. Leaving me to be hated, derided, exiled, imprisoned, raped, tortured, flayed in strips, castrated,

put to death by the sword, burned at the stake, gassed, shot, shoved into ovens, my ashes smeared over Europe.

Leaving me at my desk, at my typewriter. Leaving me in the library among floors of books as the sands of the sea. Setting me on fire with words. Throwing me into a classroom. Putting paper at my disposal and liberty in my soul, generations of voices in my ears, and they argue, and sometimes they sing. Commandment after commandment, who can obey enough, hear clearly enough. Leaving me logging in the hours, the years, it is just a lifetime and it isn't enough, it isn't forty years—reading and trying to comprehend, trying to explain. To bring twigs to the fire where children are huddling. Trying to write whatever I am supposed to write, praying for the phrases to come to me, cursing my own stupidity.

Leaving at all times a remnant telling the story, intoxicated by time future. Next year in Jerusalem. Soon the promised land.

What is the promised land, that the Almighty drives us to it. A child runs by the oceanside, dashes barefoot into the surf, runs giggling to the mother. The grandmother hitches her pruning hook over a long branch. In the evening the man under his fig tree and the man under his vine get together to discuss the next election, the wives join them and nobody makes them afraid.

Milk and honey, the desert blooms, spacious skies.

The promised land really exists, it really doesn't, are we there yet. Borders unspecified, we will know when we've arrived.

Profusely fertile, agriculturally a heartland; good also for grazing; room for cities. Are we there yet. The land of opportunity, these truths to be self-evident, it is necessarily elsewhere, from sea to shining sea. No more auction block. Take this hammer, carry it to the captain, tell him I'm gone. Emancipate yourself from mental slavery. If you are not for yourself who is for you, if you are for yourself alone what are you, and if not now, when. Keep your hand on that plow, hold on. No more sin and suffering, no pharaoh, no king, one man one vote, are we there yet, no grinding the faces of the poor, are we there yet, no bribing of judges, are we there yet.

An impossible place, let freedom ring in it. We've been to the mountain. We've seen the land: a terrain of the imagination, its hills skipping for joy. How long, we say, we know our failure in advance, nobody alive will set foot in it.

The Songs of Miriam

And Miriam the prophetess took a timbrel in her hand; and all the women went out after her with timbrels and with dances.

EXODUS 15:20

*An exile, strange to every wind,
may I be given field and fallow land . . .
my silent soul howls like the jackals
and cries out like the sea.*

YOCHEVED BAT-MIRIAM

I'm a young girl
My periods not started yet
Up to my waist in Nile water, I push
The baby basket through the bulrushes
Onto the beach
Come on, I say to myself, let's go
And they see it
And come running
My brother cries like a kitten
In the arms of that princess
Her painted face fills with the joy
Of disobedience, which is the life of joy
When she is hooked I walk
Out of the river
Bowing and bowing

I am Miriam, daughter
Of Israel

We gather the limbs, we gather the limbs
We gather the limbs of the child
We sing to the river, we bathe in the river
We save the life of the child.

If you listen to me once
You will have to go on listening to me
I am Miriam the prophetess
Miriam who makes the songs
I lead the women in a sacred circle
Shaking our breasts and hips
With timbrels and with dances
Singing how we got over
O God of hosts
The horse and his rider
Have you thrown into the sea—
That is my song, my music, my
Unended and unfinished prophecy—
The horse was captivity
And its rider fear—

O God of hosts
Never again bondage
Never again terror
O God of hosts.

Call me rebelliousness, call me the bitter sea
I peel the skin off myself in strips
I am going to die in the sand

Miriam the leprous, Miriam the hag
Miriam the cackling one
What did I have but a voice, to announce liberty
No magic tricks, no miracles, no history,
No stick
Or stone of law. You who believe that God
Speaks only through Moses, bury me in the desert
I curse you with drought
I curse you with spiritual dryness
I spit on your promise
But you who remember my music
You will feel me under your footsoles
Like cool ground water under porous stone[†]—

Follow me, follow my drum
Follow my drum, follow my drum
Follow me, follow my drum
Follow my drum.

[†] Miriam is afflicted with leprosy after she and Aaron challenge Moses' rule (Numbers 12). She dies in the desert (Numbers 20:1). Immediately afterward, there is a drought which results in Moses' being forbidden to enter the promised land. Is there a connection? Ilana Pardes proposes in *Counter-Traditions in the Bible* that all the women in the Exodus story are vestiges of the Egyptian protectress goddess Isis. Moreover, Miriam means "bitter sea," and the vestigial memory of a water-goddess (the Canaanite Asherah/Anath?) perhaps underlies the rabbinic legend of Miriam's well, which is supposed to have followed the Israelites in the desert, and dried up at her death. This was the same well over which Abraham's and Abimelech's men contended, say the sages; in the wilderness it always settled opposite the Tabernacle; the leaders of the twelve tribes with their staffs would chant to it and make it gush forth as high as pillars. The hasidim believe that all well water becomes Miriam's water as Sabbath approaches, and that a sip of this water makes one wise in Torah.

I who am maiden
woman and crone
I who am
Miriam.

The Opinion of Aaron

*And when the people saw that Moses delayed to
come down from the mount, the people gathered
themselves together unto Aaron, and said unto
him, Up, make us a god who shall go before us; for
as for this Moses, the man that brought us up out
of the land of Egypt, we know not what is become
of him.*
EXODUS 32:1

*Be of the disciples of Aaron, loving peace and
pursuing peace.*
THE WISDOM OF THE FATHERS

It is written that he was meek,
That he was a great teacher,
Moshe rabbenu. Lies. A brutal joke.
Crazy as a bedbug
Would be more like it.
He never saw God.
He hallucinated that screaming zero,
That noisy hole, it lived nowhere, it was a
Mass hallucination. Not
Even the first item did
He understand of what
People need: law and order,
Rules and regulations, something

To touch, something solid, a
Little bit of peace and quiet.
Everything else is bull. What gaiety
We felt when he disappeared
Into the roaring smoke
Pouring from the mountain,
Gone for good, we hoped—until
He struck. When I heard the bugles, when I saw
His men hack through
The chests of our sons
As if they were chickens
I thought it was the end of me.
Here, he says. Take these robes,
Gold, purple, fringed, jeweled,
Be the priest.
There is nothing
To forgive.
A scream wants to roll out of my mouth
That would strangle him and his maniac God
Forever. I swallow it like a ball of yarn
Sticky from lamb's-blood, I don't choke, only to myself
Do I reveal the priest's plan:
Never again,
No wild men,
No revelation.

History

A Midrash on Sinai

*To everything there is a season; and a time to
every purpose under the heaven.*
ECCLESIASTES 3:1

History is oxygen to Jews.
LEON WIESELTIER

*T*he rabbis tell that at Sinai when God proposed the covenant to the multitude, the multitude refused it. They
refused until God held the mountain over the heads of the
people, saying that if they accepted the covenant, good; otherwise they would find their graves under the mountain. Then
they agreed.

But others tell it that God scowled and dropped Sinai onto
Moses, who supported it on his shoulders until the moment of
his death, while the Israelites stumbled forward under its massive shadow. For those forty years when they looked up they
saw no sky, only hanging roots, raw rock. After a while they
forgot the distinction, and thought it was the sky.

And yet others declare that even after death Moses remained
unrelieved of his burden, although Sinai lightened somewhat
when the Israelites began immediately to argue over the meaning

of the Law; lightened again when David touched harpstrings and lifted up his eyes unto the hills; lightened vastly when Isaiah imagined swords hammered into plowshares; when Akiba demanded the canonical inclusion of the Song of Songs over the heads of a rabbinical committee; when Maimonides affirmed the God of the philosophers and Spinoza denied him; when semi-literate Hasidim began to dance; when Peretz wrote certain fables, and Kafka others; when Chagall having settled in Paris brightened his palette; and when Einstein puzzled and Heifetz fiddled. Today let us suppose that the mass of Sinai has decreased by the weight of a sparrow. Let it be pronounced that we are making excellent progress. We are making history.

The Sabbath
Mystery against History

Remember the sabbath day, to keep it holy.
EXODUS 20:8

*The mystery of the sabbath . . . that unites itself
through the mystery of the One. . . . And as they
unite above, so also do they unite below in the
mystery of oneness.*
THE ZOHAR

And besides, there is the Sabbath. And besides, there is the
ladder God lets down from the aperture of heaven. Lets
it cascade down, pulls it up, lets it down. And besides, there is
the Sabbath. How could it be forgotten? Bliss, then. A stab in
the ticking of the celestial mattress, a puncture so that the
softest of down feathers keeps pouring out. And light keeps
pouring out, from the wound of time, which heals at sunset but
opens six days later, pours out like blood but isn't blood. Because God rested, we are permitted to escape time and to rest
peacefully together in the shower of eternity. As above, so
below. We, and our families, and our animals, and everyone
who works, and the strangers among us. And the further we
scatter ourselves, the more this peaceful concentrated light pours
everywhere, among the nations. We catch it in the bowls of our

hands. Bliss, then. It flies into the candles. It swims in glasses of wine. We chew it in bread. We bless everything.

And besides, there is the Sabbath. It ripples from Sinai, through space and time, until this very evening.

The Story of Joshua

And Joshua said, Hereby ye shall know that the
living God is among you, and that he will without
fail drive out from before you the Canaanites, and
the Hittites, and the Hivites, and the Perizzites,
and the Girgashites, and the Amorites, and the
Jebusites.
JOSHUA 3:9

The New Englanders are a people of God settled in
those which were once the devil's territories.
COTTON MATHER, 1692

We reach the promised land
Forty years later
The original ones who were slaves
Have died
The young are seasoned soldiers
There is wealth enough for everyone and God
Here at our side, the people
Are mad with excitement.
Here is what to do, to take
This land away from the inhabitants:
Burn their villages and cities
Kill their men
Kill their women
Consume the people utterly.

God says: is that clear?
I give you the land, but
You must murder for it.
You will be a nation
Like other nations,
Your hands are going to be stained like theirs
Your innocence annihilated.
Keep listening, Joshua.
Only to you among the nations
Do I also give knowledge
The secret
Knowledge that you are doing evil
Only to you the commandment:
Love ye therefore the stranger, for you were
Strangers in the land of Egypt,† a pillar
Of fire to light your passage

---

† Deuteronomy 10:19. The first of many variations and repetitions of this commandment is Exodus 23:9, "Thou shalt not oppress a stranger: for ye know the heart of the stranger, seeing you were strangers in Egypt." The decalogue declares that sabbath rest applies to strangers as well as Israelites; a dozen texts in Exodus, Leviticus, Numbers, and Deuteronomy command equality under law for natives and strangers and forbid natives to oppress or vex the strangers among them. Abraham (Gen. 23:4) and Moses (Ex. 2:22) define themselves as strangers, and King David in Psalm 39 declares himself before God as "a stranger with thee, and a sojourner, as all my fathers were." It is a Jewish truism that the experience of being alien and oppressed teaches kindness and compassion. Yet the conquest of territory requires ruthlessness. Thus the tension (is it a division? Is it not a division?) between the values of national survival and those of universal compassion stands at the core of Jewish history in a new way with the conquest of the Land. Three thousand years later in contemporary Israel the division continues to produce anguish. A similar anguish saturates relations between "Americans" and "Native Americans."

Through the blank desert of history forever.
This is the agreement.
Is it entirely
Clear, Joshua,
Said the Lord.
I said it was. He then commanded me
To destroy Jericho.

Judges, or Disasters of War

*In those days there was no king in Israel: every
man did that which was right in his own eyes.*
JUDGES 21:25

*Turning and turning in the widening gyre,
The falcon cannot hear the falconer.
Things fall apart; the center cannot hold;
Mere anarchy is loosed upon the world.
The blood-dimmed tide is loosed, and everywhere
The ceremony of innocence is drowned.*
W. B. YEATS

The crisis center needs a paint job, which it will not receive for the foreseeable future since there is a war on and no available funds. When, we may ask, is there not a war on. What is human history but the history of that war, fought either against our neighbors or among ourselves. Therefore the plaster curls picturesquely on the ceiling. The phone bill is behind. A casement in the window was broken by a flying brick. The donated furniture is dented and wears a light coating of grease and dust. Down the street are a shoe repair shop, a butcher, a porno movie house, a diner, some warehouses. Outside the window, litter flies down the avenue like pieces of forgotten childhood learning. Inside there are flyspecked posters on the walls, a woman with a submachine gun, a woman nursing a child, an arm raised in defiance.

Several adolescent girls giggle in one corner. In another corner a pale woman in her mid-thirties with jet black hair, love beads, and bitten fingernails pours coffee into styrofoam cups, preparing for the afternoon group meeting in which some attempt is made at education. The leader tries to give the women who gather at the center a sense of personal identity and shared community. The afternoon discussions are always seething with tales, crackling with narratives. War stories, tales of horror.

Deborah tells her group the story of the Levite's concubine. Once there was a girl who fell in love with a travelling lawyer from the side of Mount Ephraim. He met her in the marketplace of Bethlehem-judah, gave her jewelry, and then bought her from her father. She travelled with him bringing her clothing and cooking things to his place. After some months, perhaps he beat her, perhaps she was merely lonely or bored, she went back to live with her father. She was sixteen. The lawyer came to fetch her home. The woman's father greeted the man as a son-in-law and feasted him for five days, with meat and wine, not permitting him to leave, hoping perhaps to keep both his daughter and the young man at his side. But finally they left. As it happened they lodged on the way in Gibeah, a Benjamite town. That night a hostile crowd of Benjamite men gathered outside the door, demanding to see the lawyer. Send him outside, they yelled drunkenly. We want to talk to him.[†]

[†] Judges 19 is a replay of the scene at Sodom, obviously; but, as Mieke Bal points out, the replay is in the context of a shift from patrilocal to virilocal possession of women, which the Benjamite men are represented as resisting. The girl *is* murdered in the story, and the Levite *is* attacked through the butchery of his property, which he then further butchers as if to re-establish control. I have followed Bal in seeing The Book of Judges as a book whose subtext is the war of the sexes, and in disregarding the supposed chronology

Some of the women in the shelter already know what will happen. Surreptitiously they watch the new girls. They know this is the story to end all stories, a real shocker, and they like to see the new girls react.

Well, says Deborah, in this case there were no angels present. First the old man who was the host offered the mob his own daughter, a maiden, along with the lawyer's woman, saying do what you want with them, humble them, but leave my guest alone, don't commit your vileness with him. And then the lawyer pushed his woman out into the street.

Around the table they picture it, they know it, how the Levite's woman fell from the doorway and looked at the mob of men. The men were licking their chops. They were laughing, elbowing. She looked at their teeth and tongues in the chalky floodlight of a cool moon. They knocked her down, tore her dress off and began to bite at her face breasts belly. Someone poured the dregs of a bottle of wine over her. Use the bottle, use the bottle, the men yelled. Someone had the thighbone of a dog to thrust into her. She called and fought and fell silent. After some hours the moon set, the sky lightened. The woman crept to her host's doorsill. She put her hands on the threshold. After a while her man opened the door following his night's sleep and gazed out at the day. Time to go, he said, but nobody answered. I hope you are all paying attention because this is a true story, says Deborah. The lawyer lay the girl's corpse over his donkey and brought it home. Then with a knife he divided it into twelve pieces and sent one piece to each of the twelve tribes of

---

of the book, which scholars assume to be its central theme but which is in fact very weakly rendered.

Israel, demanding a judgment against the Benjamites who had insulted him. The Benjamites refused to surrender the culprits, and the upshot was war, a vast slaughter of men and destruction of cities. Well, let's have some comments.

The married women are shy, looking down at the table. This is not a good moment in history. Their husbands for the most part are drunkards, or crazies, with or without the excuse of combat experience. The women visit the center from time to time, mostly all they hope for is peace, they should raise their children in good health, their husbands should quit breaking dishes, cursing in front of the children, slapping them around in public. They try to be obedient wives, for everyone says if the husband is unhappy the wife is to blame, they truly try their best. The women who have been divorced by their husbands are perhaps worse off. They remember a room of men in black, saying holy words, refusing to look at them, refusing to touch them, men without pity. And then the agunot, women who have been abandoned by their husbands and can never remarry, who become like lifeless sticks. Red hands, evasive eyes, emaciation. The whiners and the beggars, the desperate marketers of their own bodies. Voices coarsened from screaming. Each with a tale to unfold that would wither your spirit. Drowning people gasping air, Deborah thinks, what is the use, mere straws I throw them. God help us regain our womanly strength, Deborah says to herself when she regards the flotsam thrown on her cement doorsill. God help us through this age of brother fighting brother, tribe murdering tribe. Turn us, Oh Lord, prays Deborah silently. A dull-normal girl, pregnant, who never speaks at meetings, has tears running down her cheeks. The rest look at her with some contempt.

A young runaway from a wealthy family raises her hand smirking, crossing her legs under the chipped table. The plot resembles that of the Iliad, and that of the Mahabarata and Ramayana, if you're looking at epics, she says. The men always fight wars over their wounded honor with some woman as pretext. Their inflated egos is more like it. And remember Jephthah's daughter, who got sacrificed because her father, that idiot, promised to sacrifice whoever first came out of his house if he was victorious in some battle? And Jacob's daughter Dinah, who got used as an excuse for our men to murder all the men of Schechem? Did anybody for one minute care how Dinah felt about being raped?[†] No news here, she yawns. The pigs are the same everywhere. Wait, says Deborah. We are speaking of Jews not gentiles. Remember that among Jews these stories are not heroic but scandalous. A symptom of social chaos, when men forget to obey God as their Lord and King, and therefore fall into abominations. For us it is tragic when women suffer. Doesn't that prove that Jews respect women? Don't you remember our saying that the price of a virtuous woman is far above rubies? Sure, right, says the runaway. Fools grow without rain. That's why the Levite is never punished, and Jephthah is never punished, and the rabbis never condemn them. No, the stories are to make us afraid. To terrify us into submission. She glares around the table but the other women are shrinking, disinclined to meet her eyes.

Deborah thinks it is time to tell something inspirational, a story of the old days, the days of faith. She squares her massive

---

[†] The episodes of Jephthah's daughter and the rape of Dinah are in Judges 11 and Genesis 34 respectively. Rabbinical commentary typically blames Dinah for her rape. In Deena Metzger's novel *What Dinah Thought*, Dinah and Schechem are secretly married, and Dinah curses the sons of Jacob after they massacre Schechem; violence between Israelites and Schechemites (i.e., Palestinians) will plague both nations throughout history.

shoulders. Many years ago, says Deborah, my ancestress was a judge in Israel. A prophetess, a mother, and a judge. She was famous for defeating the Canaanites who oppressed us with their nine hundred iron chariots.[†] It was she under her palm tree in Mount Ephraim who mobilized our armies, she who promised our timid general Barak that she would go with him, and she who predicted that the enemy general Sisera would be killed by a woman. O my soul, thou hast trodden down strength. For the stars in their courses fought against Sisera, at the foot of Mount Tabor, and his people fell upon the edge of the sword, and not a man was left alive. Fleeing before us, Sisera stumbled into the tent of Jael, wife of Heber, thinking he would be safe there. Water, he croaked. And now hear what a heroine was this Jael. She gave him milk, she brought forth butter in a lordly dish, she covered him with a blanket and told him to sleep. Then while he slept she drove a tent stake through his head.

So perish all our enemies! Victory! Go for it, Jael! yell the women. Yes, continues Deborah, feeling herself at last a queen bee in her own hive. Yes, and think how that night the mother of Sisera looked through her lattice, wondering why Sisera was so long in arriving with his chariot. She expected him any moment to appear with his armies, having captured one or two of our Israelite women for each of his men. Boo, hiss, yell the women. They are picturing the general with the nail through his skull, they are elated with patriotism, and also something else.

For how good it is to kill, to kill in revenge. For the times they squeeze your breasts with their thick fingers. For the times they

---

[†] The story of Deborah and the defeat of Sisera is in Judges 4–5.

pretend you do not exist, while you beg them to listen to you. For the times they beat you and you creep away to wash your own blood, and make excuses for them to the children. For their indifference when you are sick and weak, although if a mosquito bites *them* they think the sky is falling. For the times they travel and forget to telephone. For the times they shit themselves, drunk, and you have to clean them. For their disgusting vomit. For their evil language, their laughter, their sarcasm, their warning index fingers. For the way they look at you with revulsion, pressing their lips together. For their joviality whenever any woman is humiliated. For their comradeship among themselves which excludes you. A nail, yes, a nail through the head, that would teach them. The women all sigh, they never have such wicked fantasies, they permit themselves a crude joke sometimes to communicate a shared fury. Why don't women have any brains? Because they don't have any pricks to put them in. They have their little litanies of grievances. He said, then I said, and then the sonofabitch had the nerve to say.

A new woman, a redhead in a black dress and gold necklaces has arrived, is standing by the door, they motion her to the table. She drinks the bad coffee with the rest and listens. Now the women are discussing personal problems, this week's bad news. They offer each other strategic advice and support. When her turn comes, the red headed woman describes her relationship with her husband. As she speaks she becomes pale and pushes her rings up and down her fingers. The man was a bully, an animal, you can't tame somebody like that except by killing him. My love was infatuation, madness, she says. How his handsome arrogance dragged her like gravity. How her enthralled nervous system would start hanging up crepe paper, flinging tinsel, flicking the strobes, when he walked into a room, even when she felt most hatred for him. The other women nod, oh sister, they know all about it. The hyperventilation express, the jungle juice special, what woman doesn't.

Yet her heart resisted, she explains. He was a brute, the enemy, not even intelligent enough to argue with, his God and his country meant nothing to him, he was just a killing machine, a criminal. Imagine a man who called himself a servant of God in one breath, then in the next breath bragged about the fights he picked, his technique of feinting at a man's head with one hand and stabbing him in the gut like lightning with the other. The stories he told! Ripping a lion apart barehanded! Killing thousands of men with the jawbone of an ass—and the men are *her* countrymen, and he was telling her this as some kind of preface to lovemaking, he was *proud* of it, his eye whites and teeth gleaming like a wolf's, he was a complete wilful *infant*. She tried not to love him. You disgust me, she said. He would go back to his own people but then he would appear again in her doorway, rippling his pectorals. And in the city of her flesh, as this destructive child approached, swaggering, the shopkeepers of her body would be flinging open doors, rolling out awnings, ripping padlocks from windows, setting forth the tempting goods.

The redhead tells her story gaspingly. I have to get some counseling, she says. I was desperate, without a choice, I was like a goddamned leaf in the wind. I even thought he was asking for it. Please help me. Please try to understand. She beats her fist against her breast, where the golden chains dangle.

One by one the women understand who the redhead is. Whore, instrument of the devil. Philistine bitch. They look at her with horror and confusion. Get out of here, says Deborah. But I did less than Jael, says the redhead, I didn't kill him. I only weakened him. All I did was cut his goddamned hair. And you must have heard that Samson was a total psychopath, murdering my countrymen, my own relatives, for nothing, just to show off his strength.[†] Please, says Delilah, looking around the shabby room, can't I stay, I really need counseling. Get out, says Deborah. And I mean now.

[†] The story is in Judges 13–16.

The Redeeming of Ruth

And Naomi said, Turn again, my daughters. . . .
And Ruth said, Entreat me not to leave thee, or to
return from following after thee: for whither thou
goest I will go; and where thou lodgest I will
lodge; thy people shall be my people and
thy God my God.
RUTH 2:11–16

Some say a host of cavalry or infantry
is the most beautiful sight
on the black earth, and some say
long ships; but I say
whomever one loves, is.
SAPPHO

Sometimes there is no war. It is like the promise. Mere normality is born, grows up like an awkward country girl whom nobody notices much until she comes home from dancing at the roadhouse, maybe, or a back seat at the drive-in movie, and she's pregnant. Now she seems a new person. Gradually she swells. The stringy hair begins to shine so she combs it. The skin clarifies, so she washes. Her stride tells you she possesses futurity in her round belly, a mischievous miracle, she's been eating the bread of boundlessness. Between wars, peace—shalom, greeting—a lump sum, a pregnant young woman, her slender feet upon the mountains, joy doubles and redoubles itself like cells in mitosis, tumbles like the fluff of cottonwoods, there is a permanently startled intelligence in every seed. You almost forget that all of life is war. History blurs a little, you can't remember your uncles' combat stories. You forget where the borders used to be. A cornfield on our side looks exactly like a cornfield on their side, the wind rustles the foliage of the woods, the guards at the checkpoints go home, their machine guns rust, they beget numerous children and on holidays they enjoy getting up early to make coffee and slice oranges for the wife. Let her sleep in, they think, rubbing their palms against their chests in morning satisfaction. They practice the clarinet, tend sunflowers in the front yard, coach the little league, polish the car until she gleams like a jewel.

Now in the drops of this most balmy time, with its unfulfillable promise and its eternal reality going hand in hand down the road, two barefoot women walk. They too are holding hands, an old widow and a young one.

At first she mistrusted me: no woman trusts her daughter-in-law. Her son having brought me home, she welcomed me politely and sourly enough. I was from the wrong class, had no manners, wore frightful clothes. She let me know it. There were honeyed offers to take me shopping. Proud of my poverty, I demurred. There were gifts of frilly nightgowns I considered absurd. What a pretty blouse you're wearing, she would say. I knew it was not.

Spoken to, I retreated from her smoker's voice, her cultivated accent, the perfume from between her fleshy breasts.

Two barefoot women, an old widow and a young one, about to bid each other farewell. Is it a trance that Ruth falls into, or what is it? Her heart, that has no proper language, appears to be giving her wordless instructions. Leave the country of your fathers and mothers. Go with your mother-in-law, Naomi, who loves you and whom you love. Do not turn back. Let her people be your people and her god your god.[†] You will come to a border. Walk across it. You will arrive under the shelter of the wings of one who is not jealous, who is not a warrior or a punisher, but a being as naturally benign as nature in a year of good harvest.

You will be a stranger, but you will meet kindness.

So Ruth takes Naomi's hand and goes. Ruth, mulling over it again and again as they walk the road to Bethlehem through the warm weather. Naomi complains, and yet I love her. A broken old woman, yet I cling to her. I would like to die and be buried with her. Greeted with joy on her return by her townspeople, Naomi announces that she is empty. Do not call me Naomi, my sweetness, but Mara, bitter, she says. It is I then who must sweeten her, thinks Ruth.

[†] Cynthia Ozick describes Ruth as a female Abraham, discovering monotheism for herself. Robert Alter notes that her story like Abraham's concerns geography and biology, the leaving of the parental house and traveling to a new country, the natural bonds yielding to new contractual bonds. Phyllis Trible notices that Ruth keeps taking initiatives she is not told to take. Is it significant that love between women is what brings the outsider,

What sweetened us: her son, my husband, who praised us to one another.

What sweetened us: she taught reading at P.S. 9 for thirty years. They sent her the ones who could not yet read in third grade, the delinquents, the immigrants, the slow. A special class. By the end of the year without exception they were reading. I'm never in trouble in this neighborhood, she said. The criminals doing business on the street are my ex-pupils, they make sure I get respect.

What sweetened us: ritual Friday nights. Chicken livers sauteed in onions, cocktails, candles, pot roast dinner, a dozen at table, shouting, politics, history, economics. I yell therefore I am, she said.

What sweetened us: the walk across Central Park to synagogue. The challenge of fasting on Yom Kippur. The crowd for Pesach. One grandmother famous a half century ago as a suffragette, another who sang quaveringly in Yiddish. The wine and gravy stained Reconstructionist Haggadahs from which we read in turn while debating the interpretation. Published in 1942, with folkloric illustrations, the text speeds past the plagues in one paragraph as if embarrassed. It dwells at length on our liberation from Egypt as a model for all struggles against tyranny and oppression. It looks forward to

---

the "stranger," into the covenant? Does the Naomi-Ruth bond repair the Sarah-Hagar split?

*a time of universal emancipation and brotherhood. And here
I am at home.*

⬚

It is harvest time when they arrive in Bethlehem. A cornfield in
Judah is like a cornfield in Moab. Ruth goes out to the fields to
glean behind the reapers.

Poppies between cornrows. Birdsong. The mystery of how that
throbbing fills the air from its tiny source, invisible—oh my
God, Ruth thinks, bending and straightening—what, anyway,
is music, why so fierce, so much greater than consolation, it
tears your breast open like a shirt, takes your throbbing heart
out, lets the heart feel fresh air bathe it—your heart the size of a
bird. And the sunball scorches it, then the song quietly returns
my heart to my body, sutures the wound, and in a moment
there's no scar.

Heat—to pull my shirt off, like the men, is what I would love. I
glean efficiently behind them, thinking the generosity of him
whose land this is. He who tells the men: let her glean, in fact be
careless in your reaping so that the stranger will not go hungry.
And I am still that stranger, wishing I might take my shirt off as
I glean, to sweat like them, I don't mind the backache, bending
and rising.

Words all stiff and wrong, foreign, if I could dance my body
would explain. Every moment a threshold. No, an opening.
The dirt road. The shack. The dome over one's head flaring,
incredible, as one stands barefoot in a cornfield, an armload of
sheaves, dust tickling one's nose. Rich and poor scattered over

the fields. The high hot cobwebby summer morning rolling by, the afternoon a cauldron. The reapers singing at work, the Hebrew rolling like a wheel. The sky turning pale, sighing, freshness of night through which like a sickle the moon rises.

(Naomi in a narrow room in the city, to whom I bring my skirtful of barley. Wide fields all around. He who blesses his workers and also his handmaiden: he is our kinsman, he is unmarried, what a coincidence, Naomi and I discuss this. What she tells me to do, I say I will do.)

⬧

Between heart attacks she campaigns for progressive candidates for Congress, teaches her special methods to young reading teachers, smokes, drinks, tells the doctors to go to hell. She is glad I am a teacher. When my daughters are born she praises their beauty and brains. You know, she says in her smoker's voice, I can only tolerate people who are attractive and intelligent. She gives us a subscription to the New York City Ballet. You walk like a dancer, she tells me. In the last year of her life we march against the war, she gives me one more nightie. My son is born in the same month that United States troops invade Cambodia. I have a photograph of her in a bathing suit, frail, looking at the bundle in her arms. May he never be a soldier, I say. Damn right, she says.

⬧

Plentiful, plentiful, the drummers drum in unison, the pipes flying alongside like a flock of sparrows accompanying an eagle. The young men and women dance tirelessly, they stamp the ground, kick, reel, spin, arms around each other's shoulders, circling and shouting. Sparks fly upward from the bonfires. I am at the edges of the circles, walking swiftly. I uncover the landowner's body in the threshing house. He wakes, bewildered. Straw in his hair. A large thick body one must admire for its lingering strength, through which sadness courses like brine. Kindly eyes in their network of wrinkles. Rich, honest, gentle, childless man. I am like the sheaves, filled with nourishment, lying at his feet. Do I know that I am beautiful? Yes, naturally, my beauty is my language; with it I converse with Boas. Generous middle-aged Boas will possess my youth. Will protect me. Cover me with his skirt, his wings. I am a stranger yet am also a bridge. I am the erasure of borders. I am ready to be redeemed. My name is Ruth, daughter-in-law of your kinswoman the Hebrew Naomi who loves me and whom I love. I am Ruth the Moabitess. I shall be Ruth the root.[†] Women shall call me better than seven sons. I bring joy to your house.

[†] Ruth will be grandmother of Jesse who will be the father of King David. As a Moabitess she is descended from one of Lot's daughters who lay with Lot incestuously—"Moab" means "from the father"—and indeed Ruth's seduction of the paternal Boas (who calls her "daughter") is like an idyllic pastoral replay (redemption?) of the story of Lot's daughters. For Torah loves the breaking of boundaries, we see it again and again.

Hannah, or Sons and Lovers

Now there was a certain man . . . and he
had two wives; the name of the one was Hannah,
and the name of the other Peninah:
and Peninah had children,
but Hannah had no children.
I SAMUEL I:I-2

What do women want?
SIGMUND FREUD

What do women want? Dear God, what do they want? To have sons. It boils down to sons. Name your civilization, when it comes to roles for women, they tend to simmer down fast to the propagation of sons. Especially when a son is the only access to power.

Hannah comes late in the narratives of barren women. It is as if the Book remembers the usefulness of that image from its distant childhood. Ah yes: the barren wife, the power of God over fertility, the value of an episode of divine intervention to establish political legitimacy.

The twist is that Hannah herself intervenes. The husband loves her devotedly, no problem there. Am I not better than ten sons to you, he asks. Well, no. For there is a second wife, who spits out children like a rabbit. A goat. Hannah therefore in bitterness of soul sojourns to a temple in the suburbs where she prays silently for a (not child but) man child, vowing that if God grants this prayer, she will dedicate the infant to his service.

I imagine Hannah's tormented prayer: You tell us to increase and multiply yet you prevent me. You make me a shadow, a void, a rottenness, my pointed breasts a shame, my gleaming fur a living starvation. How can you do this. Give me, give me, give me a son to take away my emptiness. I swear I will give him back.

She prays in pain, but silently. Eli the priest thinks she is drunk and tries to throw her off the premises. When she tells him her tale, he relents and wishes her well. And so Hannah mates an old story with a new one. For hers is the honor of inaugurating private prayer and thus a new form of piety.[†]

Nail it down. Woman to God, direct communication, God back to woman. The third term will be Samuel, Shem-El, God's name. Samuel himself has little to say in the matter. Yes, he will be born. When he is weaned, Hannah delivers him to the temple. What Mother Sarah loses—control of her own beloved son—Hannah appears to repossess. Or perhaps we should understand that Hannah preemptively thrusts Samuel out of his family and into his public role, as an employee might say you

---

[†] It is said that the Amidah, the silent prayer at the center of the Hebrew liturgy, is modelled on Hannah's prayer.

can't fire me, I quit. To control a son is still to surrender him, to surrender is to control. For if women exist to produce sons, sons exist to sustain the covenant.

⚘

What I wanted was everything. At least one of everything. We had a daughter. Then another daughter. We tried again and had a son. At that time, my country, that is myself, was daily bombing the mountains and valleys of Vietnam, and had recently invaded its neighbor, Cambodia. Routinely what we dropped on Asian villages was napalm, a jellied form of gasoline designed to cling to human skin and bubblingly burn it. Other routine activities during this war included the defoliation of forests and the recreational killing of herds of elephants by American flyers, and the rape, torture, and murder of civilians by American ground troops.

I lived in the first century of those wars, wrote the American Jewish poet Muriel Rukeyser. Most mornings I would be more or less insane.

At the end of World War II I was still a child. I sat on my father's shoulders for a Victory in Europe Day parade, like a child. However, I recall thinking not only how horrible war was, but how stupid, how irrational. When the United Nations was founded I recall thinking, with joy and relief, that nationalism would die now.

When my son was born, I too vowed something. It was evident that sons throughout history were expected to be soldiers. The mother was required to carry the son in her body, bring him into the world, cherish him until he was old enough to kill/be killed, and then surrender him to the military. I vowed that my son would not, if I could help it, be a soldier or a violent man. I hoped he would be a gentle person and good lover. I wanted to love him in a way which would increase and multiply, a ripple effect, when he undertook his life in the world. This too I suppose was a form of control, a mother trying to influence the course of history through her son.

Samuel emulates the model of piety and control provided by Hannah. Like Jewish mother, like Jewish son. This is a boy who gets into no trouble, does his homework, obeys his elders, will be famous for correctness. As priest he replaces the sons of Eli who have collapsed into corruption. Under his leadership all Israel returns to the worship of God, the people put away their idols, the yoke of the Philistines is thrown off. He judges Israel for decades, the Lord not permitting his words to drop to the ground. Unfortunately his own sons, as he grows old, grow corrupt; so the people decide they want a king like the other nations. Samuel warns them against the evils of monarchy, reminds them that God is their true monarch, points out that they need no other, but they insist. And so it is Samuel who anoints Saul first king of Israel, and it will be Samuel who sternly rebukes Saul when he goes astray. He will tell Saul that God hates him. He will anoint David. He will be very firm on the subjects of obedience and righteousness.

Like his sisters, he rejected Hebrew school. We were parents of a permissive philosophy; if the children said no, it was no. At eleven he announced his desire for a bar mitzvah.

It seemed a mysterious desire, since he was neither studious nor materialist. He nagged us until we found a Hillel tutor, in exchange for which I promised to attend Hillel services weekly with my son. There I had the opportunity to argue over interpretations of scripture with other opinionated people. And so the son in this case led the mother to the fold, instead of the reverse.

We were taking a recess from Rosh Hashonah services, sitting on the concrete rim of a reflecting pool, when he asked what one had to do to be a real Jew. I pointed out that Martin Buber says there is no single correct path to worship but that each Jew must listen to his inner voice, which is God speaking within him, to guide his path. What's an inner voice, asked my son reasonably. The question stopped me briefly. It's what you were listening to, I said, when you decided you wanted a bar mitzvah and nagged us until we arranged it. Presumably that was God speaking to you. My son took this, as Henry James would say, in. He paused a moment. He nodded.

We were both surprised. Yet I believe to this day that it was God speaking inside my son. To this day I believe that it was my son listening.

As soon as they produce their children, most of the women in the stories disappear. Are disappeared. Even Ruth. Of Hannah this is not quite true. When she brings the infant Samuel to the temple, Hannah sings a long, tremendous psalm in which she praises the Lord for casting down the arrogant and uplifting the humble. He raises the poor from the dust, and lifts the beggar from the dunghill, she sings, and makes them inherit the throne of glory. (The conception of this song will float, independent of history, until it is reuttered by Isaiah and other prophets; reuttered in the Magnificat of Mary; and uttered again in the sermon on the mount. God as the being who empowers the powerless. What an idea.)

She also comes every year to bring the child Samuel a coat she has made, as if she were a real person. And she bears three more sons and two daughters, back in her own life.

David the King

I shall be gracious unto whom I shall be gracious . . .
EXODUS 33:19

*And he sent, and brought him in. Now he was
ruddy, and withal of a beautiful countenance, and
goodly to look to. And the Lord said, Arise, anoint
him: for this is he.*
1 SAMUEL 16:12

S ome have it, some don't. Magic, charisma, giftedness,
perfection. The world is burdened with inequalities, and
there are those who appear to us to dance through it spontaneously, simply because we believe that no degree of calculation
could achieve their level of success. Even when we see them
plotting, standing over the charts making notes, or manipulat-
ing some innocent fool with an encouraging phrase and snow-
drop smile, it still seems like magic. Even if the fool is found
later with a knife under his fifth rib. If they glance up from the
legion of their admiring friends for a fraction of a second, to
wink in our direction, we are feverishly happy all day long.

It was like that in grade school. They, they—the traffic lights
always green for them. The policeman always looking the other
way. The teacher gave them the gold stars unaware it was they
who set the cat on fire. Or aware, maybe. . . . They don't need a
fancy car, or a motorcycle, or expensive clothes to make the

other guys love them, or girls either. They have a line but it isn't just that. It is just that they are perfect. They love to gamble. Hey, they say, don't you want to play? They win, whether they cheat or don't cheat. Some call it luck. If they yell *Come on, boys, over the top, let's go,* then you go.

So much success. Is it fair, after all? For one man to have everything, be everything. Undefeated athlete musician warrior popular hero crafty politician tireless lover. Founder of his dynasty and father of his country, impulsive sinner and (say the rabbis) saint.[†] Never to make an unforgivable error. When he sins, to receive a slap on the wrist from an indulgent God who has obviously decided beforehand to cherish him no matter what—though the same God punishes poor Saul with madness for a trivial misstep.

Is it fair? A fighter, a poet, incompatible vocations fused. Is it an instinct—for showmanship? Think of his first public appearance. He has arrived at the battleground bringing extra blankets from home for his brothers, who are soldiers. He himself is still a boy. He has volunteered to fight Goliath, he has been given the king's own armor—but no, it is uncomfortable for him, he will fight naked, or in sweat pants. Two armies stand watching. From a convenient stream he takes five smooth stones. The stones are just there, cool water trickling by them,

---

[†] Midrash, elaborating on the life of Israel's greatest hero, extols both David's physical strength and his poetic genius ("while still dwelling in his mother's womb he recited a poem"). The rabbis also invent for him a love of Torah and scholarship. According to the stories, the Angel of Death was powerless over David because "his mouth did not cease from learning" even while he was on his deathbed; he had to be trapped into interrupting his study in order for death to take him.

reeds growing up between them, they have been waiting patiently in the manner of stones since the early paleolithic: choose me; no, choose me. Five smooth stones, we ourselves can imagine weighing them in our palm, rinsing the mud off, rubbing the surface with our thumb.

One among them pale, oval, almost sculptural, with streaks or stars of pearl.

Some among them pale, some slate, some saffron or amber or rose. Solid colors, speckled ones, grained, spotted, striped. Basalt, granite, quartz, sandstone. Lustrous and shapely. Barefoot at the water's edge, enchanted by the forms and colors of the wet stones, I am compelled to fill my pockets with this one and that one, a dozen or more, even knowing that stones lose their lustre when they dry. Arranged on my bookshelf, their diminished beauty will continue to remind me of their original beauty.

The rest is unimaginable, to us, until it occurs. His crisp adolescent figure assuming a dancer's haughty pose instead of a fighter's, over against the giant's crouch, so that both armies must understand he has no experience of combat. Next, his defiant shout that he is about to behead the giant and leave his carcass to the birds of the air and the beasts of the field. That the battle is the Lord's, who needs no spear or shield, that the earth will see there is a God in Israel. We all hear this. Followed by his running straight toward Goliath, and before anyone knows what is happening he takes a stone from his bag, slings it on the run, it goes right through the center of the giant's forehead. Perfection.

Since he lacks a sword it is with the giant's own sword that he cuts his head off, again in a single motion which is of the greatest intensity yet somehow careless. The brute's blood squirts brightly from the fat pipelike vein in his neck. The boy yanks the head off by its dirty hair, raises it high enabling both armies to see it. At this point the men of Israel and Judah with a mighty roar chase the Philistines from the battlefield, pursue them yelling to their camp in the hills, killing multitudes of them along the way. Then we loot the Philistine tents and march home sweating and elated.

How did he do it, he did it, turned us around, the mob of us, from doubt and defeat to unity and victory. We will remember it forever. The force in our legs when we rush against our enemy. The joy in our sword grip. A flash of comprehension passes suddenly among us: what each of us has now experienced for a few moments (my arm is strong and coordinated, my aim is certain, my heart is fearless) is the holy spirit of David, our leader.

David who is whole, who is chosen, who is blessed, who is ours. David our rock.

But we need to backtrack. For to appreciate the artistry of the story, which in fact is identical in this case with its spiritual and political significance,[†] we must be completely conscious of the

---

[†] Robert Alter remarks that "The author of the David stories stands in basically the same relation to Israelite history as Shakespeare stands to

effect of contrast. The contrast, that is, between the successful boy and his shadow, the tormented one. The one we tease, the big foolish one who always does things wrong, and gets caught and punished. We must also remember that Israel has been intermittently at war with its stronger neighbors for decades, and that like a typical young nation in the absence of tyrannical control it has been disorderly, disunited, violence-ridden, and corrupt almost continuously since its conquest of the holy land. Consequently it feels a desperate need for order, as well as for a hero to whom it can open its heart in love. Such a hero could never be Saul.

At court God is afflicting King Saul with an evil spirit. Saul is suffering fits of depression. In other words he is insane, as you would be too if you were an ordinary mediocre person God had decided to favor for a while and then to abandon permanently. Through no fault of his own, or only a minor human fault, as Saul thinks. God commanded him to slaughter everyone and everything after some battle and he kept some of the animals alive and didn't kill the captured Amalekite king. It was a misunderstanding, wasn't it? Somebody *else* was responsible, it was the army who neglected to make sure all animals were dead. Anyway he was *going* to kill the animals. Wasn't it just a misunderstanding? But God means to make some sort of object lesson out of Saul. God is angry that Israel wanted a king in the first place like other nations. He warned them this would be a mistake. Now he will show them. But didn't God pluck poor Saul from obscurity himself, didn't he select him for the prophet Samuel to anoint? Saul, eager to please but not very intelligent.

English history in his history plays." Perhaps Shakespeare modeled his sense of the interplay among personality, nationality, and spirituality, on biblical narrative, as much as on Plutarch or Holinshed.

Why did God choose him if he knew he would be inadequate? Pouring his spirit upon Saul then "repenting" and withdrawing it, and Saul confessing his sin begging forgiveness tearing Samuel's robe but Samuel rebuking him saying God has now torn the kingdom away from you and won't change his mind "for he is not a man that he should repent," and isn't that inconsistent but Saul too simple to protest his mind looping he knows only all is lost.

Meanwhile God orders Samuel to fill his horn with oil and visit the house of Jesse where God will show him the new king. We remember that the house of Jesse descends from Ruth the Moabitess. However, we are to learn nothing about David's own mother or childhood. The future King David springs into existence during a familiar folklore scene: seven older brothers are rejected by God, the youngest brother is sent for. David is the chosen one, Samuel anoints him to replace Saul, and the spirit of God is with him from that day forward and forever. David is God's mirror. If God plays I'm-here-I'm-gone with his favorite, he will always fondly return.

Now back to poor mad Saul. Unlike Macbeth he had no aspirations to be king, he was plucked from his grassy hillside. He has no qualifications except his size, head and shoulders bigger than any of the people, and innocence. A country hunk, not the stuff of rulership. Also unlike Macbeth he has no illusions, he knows God has abandoned him. God hates you, says Samuel, who apparently enjoys sticking the righteous knife in. But Saul is still king. Still trying to be king. Poor Saul, grinning like a crocodile in his robes, on his throne, in the universal void. Hapless discoverer of the sickness unto death, trying to pretend that all is normal. Keeping up appearances while Hamlet

Kierkegaard and Kafka play a devil's trio in his skull. Or, worse, silence drops down on him like a ton of cement, endless silence in which his mind loops.

His advisors counsel music therapy, his servants fetch a certain boy known to be musically gifted. Saul loves David and soon makes him his armor-bearer. When the boy plays the harp, it alleviates the king's madness, his music is irreproachably healthy. *O Lord our Lord, how excellent is thy name in all the earth,* sings the boy, and Saul's heart leaps with happiness. Yes, it's true, Saul feels how excellent God is. When the boy sings of the triumphs of the Lord, Saul shifts on his throne, begins to relax, recalls his own victories, lets himself think after all maybe everything is all right, maybe Samuel was making a mistake. The boy touches his harp and his fresh voice soars like a thrush, *When I consider thy heavens, the work of thy fingers, the moon and the stars, which thou hast ordained; What is man, that thou art mindful of him? And the son of man, that thou visitest him?* The king's eyes fill with tears. *For thou hast made him a little lower than the angels, and hast crowned him with glory and honour,* and the king himself feels like a child again, yes on the hills at chilly dawn with his father's flock, and at the same time like a proud glorious man the crown on his head, the people cheering him, yes and he knows he is safe inside God's hand.

Then the madness returns, in a more virulent form. For others fall in love with David, many others. The king's daughter Michal loves him and marries him. Jonathan the king's son loves David as his own soul, with a love surpassing the love of woman. He gives David his clothes to wear, he keeps swearing fidelity. And the people, of course the people are enchanted with David their savior. Likewise the women of the people.

After every battle they dance in the street play instruments sing to each other: *Saul has killed his thousands, but David his ten thousands.*

So Saul begins to try to kill David. Twice he hurls a javelin at the young man while he is playing the harp but David escapes. *The Lord is my rock, and my fortress, and my deliverer.* Once he sends men to murder David in his bed but Michal has warned him in advance so that he escapes through a window. *Surely goodness and mercy shall follow me.* He sends messengers to capture David, but Jonathan secretly meets him in a field, they weep together, Jonathan advises him to flee. David demands to know if he has ever committed any wrong, Jonathan says of course not, Jonathan again promises deathless fidelity. Finally David goes forth into the mountains and begins to gather his own band of soldiers—the poor, the discontented, the distressed. It is now for these that he composes his psalms. *I have seen the wicked in great power, and spreading himself like a green bay tree.* So sings David, accompanied by his troops. *Make a joyful noise unto God, O ye lands.* Light from their campfire reddens the cliff face, makes the tamarind shadows dance, falls on the stone in David's hands.

🐚

Marble: limestone which has been compressed over a period of tens of thousands of years, the limestone itself having been formed from the fossil shells of myriad tiny sea organisms. It is the only stone that once was alive. The regions in which it is found were once sea floors. Its qualities of semi-opacity and sheen when polished as well as its workability make it a chosen material for architects and sculptors. The

architect often selects tinted or streaked stone for an attractive
polychromatic effect in the facades, walls, or floors of palaces,
basilicas, cathedrals, and temples. For figurative sculpture,
slabs of pure white stone are preferred as a rule.

The wars against the Philistines continue but at the same time
there is civil war of a sort. David and his small army raid foes in
border towns, they live at large in the mountains and hills, in
forests and caves, they take tribute from Abigail the wife of
Nabal, they ally themselves with the king of Gath to fight his
enemies, they defeat the Amalekites.

On the move. *Save me, O God; for the waters are come in unto my*
soul.

Criminals according to Saul, who hunts them in between his
battles with Philistines, crying that nobody is loyal to him
everyone is betraying him. One imagines his troops tire of
hearing this. Yet David according to the narrative remains
blameless. Once when out campaigning, Saul goes to "cover his
feet," Hebrew euphemism for taking a shit, inside a cave where
David is hiding. Now you can get him, say David's men. But
David only cuts a piece from Saul's garment—and afterward
goes out on the hillside and calls the king—Do you see this, the
Lord delivered you into my hand so that I could have killed
you, as my friends advised, but I will not sin against the Lord's
anointed. And what is my father the king hunting, a dead dog, a
flea? A perfect example of David's righteousness, his innocence, and his modesty. Simultaneously a perfect example of
public image making. Two armies stand watching, on a bare

stony hillside, their right hands ready to clasp their weapons, the wind riffling their hair. The guerrillas against the large conventional army. Behind all the soldiers the cave in the cliff wall, penumbra, like the entry into a man's guts. Inside the cave the residue of a stink. And Saul breaks down weeping with remorse, promises never to attack David again. It is not a promise he is able to keep. Poor mad Saul, the loose cannon. *Be thou exalted, O God, above the heavens. They have digged a pit for me, into the midst whereof they are fallen themselves.* Another story tells that David sneaks down and steals his spear one night when Saul's army is asleep in a field—and again makes his speech in the morning, and Saul is again awash with guilt.

Humiliation and self-destruction on one side of the scale. *Hide me from the secret council of the wicked.* Magnanimity and confidence on the other. *The Lord upholdeth all that fall, and raiseth up all those that be bowed down.* Remark in every anecdote an audience. Notice the instinctiveness of all his acts. No cogitation, no breast-beating, unlike Saul, unlike us. No apparent anxiety, no emotional sweat, although his life is in constant danger. If uncertain what to do on any given occasion—shall I fight, shall I flee—he simply asks God and God advises him. *Day unto day uttereth knowledge.*

But finally Saul dies in battle, along with Jonathan, after a shattering sequence of humiliations. For on the eve of a crucial engagement, outnumbered by the Philistine army which he sees approaching, he implores God for advice. Silence. The silence of God. In terror Saul seeks out a sorceress to raise the spirit of the dead Samuel—tell me what to do, he begs—and Samuel as might have been expected gives him one last cruel self-righteous lecture reminding him that God hates him. Tomorrow, announces Samuel grimly, you will be with me, you along with your sons and your army. At this Saul faints with fear. The sorceress revives him bringing him food which he at first waves away although he has not eaten for twenty-four hours. His servants and the woman compel him to get off the floor, sit on her bed and eat. And so for Saul the following morning is his last on earth. He fights up on the forested slopes of Gilboa in a frame of mind we can all too easily imagine. Or perhaps we cannot imagine it. Amid the silence of God and the shrieks of soldiers in combat, he sees three sons including Jonathan killed. Wounded himself, he asks his armor-bearer to slay him but the boy refuses; so Saul falls on his own sword and dies.

Now we cut to David's camp, three days later: a young Amalekite comes panting with the news that Saul and Jonathan are dead. He carries Saul's crown as proof, and claims to have slain Saul himself at the wounded king's request. We all comprehend that he expects a reward. But David immediately commands one of his soldiers to kill this Amalekite who has dared to touch the Lord's anointed. He then rends his clothes and bursts into the famous torrent of lamentation. *How are the mighty fallen! Tell it not in Gath, publish it not in the streets of Ashkelon, lest the daughters of the Philistines rejoice, lest the daughters of the uncircumcised triumph. Ye mountains of Gilboa, let there be no dew, neither let there be rain upon you. . . . From the blood of the slain, from the fat of the mighty, the bow of Jonathan turned not back, and the sword of Saul returned not empty. Saul and Jonathan were lovely and pleasant in their lives, and in their death they were not divided: they were swifter than eagles, they were stronger than lions. Ye daughters of Israel, weep over Saul, who clothed you in scarlet . . . I am distressed for thee, my brother Jonathan: very pleasant hast thou been to me: thy love to me was wonderful, passing the love of women.*

The event itself, a powerful story of brutality, pathos, generosity, certain to be told and retold, makes an excellent vehicle to increase popular excitement over David's personality while simultaneously advancing the innovative concept of "the Lord's anointed." Then the speech, the language. Magnificent, soaring—but separate, if you can, the eloquence of David's lamentation from its sublime irony. Distinguish the celebration of Saul's military glory from the emphatic point that Israel is now in desperate need of a fighting monarch able to hold off the Philistines. If you can, disentangle David's erotic memory of Jonathan from the idea that Jonathan would himself have chosen David as King. Divide passion from politics in the mouth of this young man—you cannot, they are flesh of flesh and bone of bone.

Nor dare you cynically criticize. If the survival of your people surrounded by enemies is desirable, David is desirable. And if you pity Saul, recall it is through David's tongue that you remember Saul's bravery and victories, David whose praise creates death's dignity, David whose wholeness emanates from him and still heals.

So they make him king over Judah the southern kingdom. For seven years then there is conflict between Judah and Israel, throughout which David's conduct is irreproachable: as always he turns to God for all decisions. If rivals must be killed it is conveniently by someone else's hand, not David's. The tales continue to multiply, the people admire him more and more. Finally David's chief rival is treacherously murdered by his own captains, they anoint David king in Israel, and he conquers Jerusalem where he builds the city of David. A wall, towers, a palace. He will fill the palace as a king should with wives, concubines, sons, daughters, servants, generals, advisors, courtiers. And scribes, let us not forget scribes. He will reign over the united kingdom for thirty-three years until the day of his death, the Lord God of hosts being with him. Now we are in deed as well as theory a nation like other nations, territorially extended from Dan to Beersheba, with its government modelled on Canaanite royal cities, with diplomatic alliances including a pact with the Phoenicians, and the influence of its empire reaching from the Nile to the Euphrates.

🔯

Like other theatrical warrior heroes. Caesar, Alexander, Napoleon, whom their soldiers venerate as leaders and fighters able to share the harsh life of the common troops. About whom stories circulate regarding their wit their eloquence their political shrewdness their generosity to allies their ferocity to enemies their noble ideals.

Charlemagne, half a bandit until he unifies Europe. Christian against Saracen. A backward patch of the globe wipes the sleepy mucus from its eyes, stumbles toward civilization. The song of Roland, stirring tale of comrades-in-arms, echoing horn among the pastoral bloodsoaked hills. Blow, bugles, blow, set the wild echoes flying. Blow, bugles; and answer, echoes, dying, dying, dying. Chivalry means, originally, this: the

*manly love of (conquest-hungry) comrades, the galloping
adventure stories of soldiers loyal unto death. Charlemagne's
empire, briefly humane, enlightened, collapses within a
century.*

*Ashoka of central India, conquering general converted to
philosophical Buddhism, promulgator of the first humane law
code on that continent. Rowdy Prince Hal, future Henry V of
England, as invented by himself, or the popular imagination
of England, or the playwright William Shakespeare. A charm-
er, a calculating cold fish, a rebel-dutiful son. Later the
legitimate conquering hero, victor at Agincourt. We few, we
happy few, we band of brothers, he cries to the troops before
battle. For God and Prince Harry, they roar responsively.*

*And David. Whoever is managing David's career is inspired.
Screenplay, sets, costumes, camerawork, casting, direction.
Photomontage of genius. Even the soundtrack is perfect, with
its combination of eloquent chanting to the delicate harp,
battle shrieks and death moans, drums and timbrels. Someone
has made certain, by brilliant editing of this material, that
David's phraseology will be repeated and recorded verbatim,
his behavior reported in minute detail, his virtues and sins
will enter the public record forever, the simple to interpret
them in their simplicity, the subtle to read between the lines in
their subtlety. The artist is (do we have a choice, reader): a
committee of scribes, the popular imagination of Israel,
David himself, or the Holy One, Blessed be He, whose goodness
endureth continually.*

*The enigma of leadership. The enigma of self-creation. The
enigma of art.*

Now the story moves into another gear. To conquer territory and popular sentiment is easier than retaining them. What can he do, being king, to sustain the adoration we felt when he was a youth and an outlaw? In addition of course to subduing our enemies, creating an empire with garrisons as far as Damascus, and receiving goodly quantities of gold and silver from foreign kings.

It is true that he has our desires on his side. If he did not exist we would invent him, he is so beautiful. We want to love him. We want to be in awe, looking from our windows, throwing the confetti—here they come, you can hear the band—we're the mob in the street, squeezed shoving peering—can you see the honor guard, the mounted police, the pretty girls on the floats throwing flowers, the geezer veterans walking out of step, the flags, the official limousines . . . no, none of that, not this time. This parade is only unarmed soldiers, we're temporarily at peace. Ranks of them go by marching briskly. But then, my God, here it is: the Ark in which God actually dwells, which the soldiers are bringing home to Jerusalem in a cart, a wooden box with curtains, if anyone accidentally touches it they burn to ashes. Up from the morning desert the men have marched, dust streaks their legs, they swing through the Dung Gate, along a stone street between rows of low houses, then past the massive dwellings of the wealthy where noblewomen and their servants shout welcome from ornamented balconies, to the marketplace where the entire populace gathers. And in front of the Ark comes the King. Almost naked. As if he had fused in a mature manly beauty the body of innocent Adam, Jacob the wrestler, the fair Joseph. Playing the harp and dancing with all his might. Leaping, jumping.

Utterly abandoned.

There follows a sardonic interchange with his wife, Michal, daughter of Saul, who has been watching from a palace window. She dislikes his exhibitionism. Showing his privates in public is vulgar. How glorious was the King of Israel today, uncovering himself in front of the handmaids of his servants, Michal remarks when she gets him alone. So you think I'm shameless, that's too bad, he says. I'm playing before the Lord, who as you recall took away your father's throne and gave it to me. I expect to be even more vile in future. The servants and handmaids like it if you don't.

Whereupon David banishes Michal for her sharp tongue, she can spend the rest of her days weeping and go to her grave childless; take a lesson, ladies. Yes, and don't we like that, his passion, pride, swiftness, don't we wish we too. . . . So that the anecdotes continue to crystallize around his virility, wonderful bits to tell and retell, to polish like a smooth stone. . . . Don't we love the David and Bathsheba story—royal lust unpunished, what a man to make our eyes sparkle vicariously, what a randy goat to set the painters painting.[†] King on the roof sees officer's

---

[†] Next to "David and Goliath," "David and Bathsheba" has been the Davidic subject most appealing to the popular imagination both within and outside of Judaism. Biblical commentary, moreover, often cites this episode as demonstration of the realism of the biblical chroniclers: although David is the paramount hero of Israel he is described warts and all. Pursuing my notion that the narrative has been designed to make David a maximally attractive figure for his own and future times, I can think of several reasons

wife in garden below taking a bath, send that one over. When Bathsheba informs the king of her pregnancy he sends for her husband who is at the front, feasts him and suggests he spend the night with his wife. We get the idea, but the patriotic husband refuses. Then he orders the husband back to the war zone where the action is hottest, with secret instructions to the commanding officer to make sure the man gets killed in action, a very bad sin surely, but when Nathan the prophet rebukes him in God's name he admits guilt humbly. What would you say of a rich man with exceeding flocks and herds who stole a poor man's one ewe lamb that he nourished up with his own hand and fed at his own table, asks Nathan. As the Lord liveth, such a man should surely die, responds David angrily. Thou art the man, says Nathan. David immediately therefore turns to God in prayer. *Have mercy upon me, O God, according to thy loving-kindness: according unto the multitude of thy tender mercies blot out my transgressions. Against thee, thee only have I sinned, and done this evil in thy sight: A broken and a contrite heart, O God, thou wilt not despise.* Well done, King. Some of us might suppose the sin against Bathsheba's husband Uriah was more glaring than the sin against God in this particular case, but David

---

for including rather than censoring the Bathsheba episode. First, it is an excellent story in itself. Second, people enjoy a bit of spicy wickedness in high places, too much virtue in a ruler is boring and oppressive (cf. Moses), his sinning actually enhances David's reputation as a "real man" (i.e., virile) and a "complete man" (i.e., one-who-has-tasted-everything), rather than detracting from him. Finally, certain historical events occurred during David's reign which might have damaged David's aura of glory and constant good fortune: the death of a child born to a new and favorite wife, the shaming of David when Absalom publicly takes his concubines, and the fact that his rule never achieves permanent peace. The explanation is that these are David's punishments for his act of sin, and were all foretold by the prophet Nathan.

evidently has his divine priorities straight. After which he marries Bathsheba. And there is also a sequel. When their newborn
child sickens as God had foreordained, David weeps and fasts,
lies on the ground, refuses to get up, but at news of the child's
death he rises, washes, prays and changes clothes, sits down for
lunch. Courtiers shocked and confused ask why; the king replies he fasted while the child was sick because you never know,
God may choose to be gracious, but there is no point fasting for
a dead child. "Can I bring him back again? I shall go to him, but
he shall not return to me." Good line, King. Terse, practical, a
bit breathtaking.

But nothing compared with the one-liner crowning the episode
of Absalom's rebellion, late in David's career.

Absalom, David's son, handsomest man in Israel and deeply
loved by his father, plots the king's overthrow. In the ugly
prehistory of this story the king's son Amnon has violently
raped the king's daughter Tamar. Absalom has sheltered Tamar
and, after waiting two full years, he has trapped Amnon at a
sheepshearing feast and killed him. Then Absalom has lived in
exile three years, although David longs to pardon him and is
finally persuaded to do so. Then he has lived in Jerusalem but
without permission to see the king's face. At last the son and
father are reconciled, the one bowing to the ground and the
other kissing him. Immediately after this reconciliation Absalom
commences his treachery.

He makes himself popular with the masses the way David used
to before he was king, giving speeches at the city gates promis-
ing to end corruption and injustice. It is the old story of youth
and age, the turning wheel. Absalom collects an army of dissi-

dents in Hebron, David flees Jerusalem with his followers. David camps in the hills while Absalom occupies the palace and makes a public demonstration of appropriating David's concubines. Ah, we remember: Nathan predicted this, a punishment for the Bathsheba affair. David places his faith in God as usual to do with him as he will. Since God helps those who help themselves, David also sends a spy to Absalom's court, to give Absalom bad military advice under cover of friendship, and to notify the king's friends of rebel army plans. When the battle is joined at Ephraim, David warns his men to avoid killing the young man Absalom. So goes the story. But of course the inexperienced Absalom is killed and the rest of his army scattered. And when David receives the news of Absalom's death he retreats to his chamber weeping. He refuses to reassume the monarchy for days, for weeks, until his advisors rebuke him. Weeping, mourning, as if the bottoms of the deeps had delivered themselves up. "O my son Absalom! my son, my son Absalom! would God I had died for thee, O Absalom, my son, my son!"

Breathtaking. Human, more-than-human. As the philosopher does not say. *This* (in our hearts we know, no philosopher can deprive us) is a man. Is totally a human being. Uncensored, free, experiencing and expressing everything. Feeling, from the bald apex of absolute victory, the subterranean truth of absolute grief. We too, if only we . . . this white stone, larger than life, more sublime more alive, shaking us because of its perfect splendor . . . heat, cold. . . .

Further battles, further politics. Now his captains fight, but not David. They recognize that he is a middle-aged man, they don't want to take the chance of his getting hurt.

Finally cold. Naturally. An aged man is but a paltry thing. Word goes through the tapestried court, the stone kitchen, out into the spring countryside. Imagine him in bed, covered with blankets, shivering. The court runs an all-Israel beauty contest, the winning virgin gets to try and warm him, it doesn't help. Poor Abishag, moist uneaten plum. David's last official act is political: he secures the throne for his chosen son Solomon. His last words are bloody minded: he advises Solomon what enemies to murder. Cold, man. And dead as stone.

♲

Not exactly a swagger, but a cool youthful poise, balanced on the one hip, the knee bones shapely, the penis and balls emerging from their nest of marble curls like tender firm fledglings, the curve of torso agreeable as a slender tree. In the muscular arms a balance between delightful relaxation and delightful tension; the hands like some overgrown boy's paws only veined and powerful as a man's. The neck a tower, the blank face turned slightly sideways looking somewhere far away. Not gold but white; white on the inside as well, hard stone through and through. Having waited inside its cliff since the early paleolithic, hardening. The sculptor age twenty-six, having completed the piece on commission for the city of Florence.

I know he is there waiting but at first I do not want to look. I prefer to approach gradually, deferring the climax of the visit. Come slowly—Eden—I murmur to myself in the words of a poet. The gallery curators have arranged unfinished marble figures by the same sculptor along the wide corridor. The warm tones of immense Flemish tapestries on the walls, rich

with images, provide their background. Each figure a repre-
sentation of human pathos combined with mineral indiffer-
ence, the marble in each case has been partially carved away
from the idea waiting inside it. The figures are prisoners,
never to pull themselves free of the white weight. And this one
is a Christ already dead, a dead weight, his knees buckled, the
muscled central body useless, ropes around his loins he has no
genitals, the head fallen sideways, two who are still alive
support him under the armpits but they too are imprisoned
forever, melting back into the stone, the steady chisel marks.

Look at each, walk slowly, give it time. Try not to be distract-
ed by the other tourists. Their innocent polylingual babble
collectively booming up and down the gallery, their flashbulbs
flashing despite the signs that forbid it. Slowly, that's right.
Now look at him, he is at the end of the corridor at the dome.

Alone. Nude. Larger than life, so much taller than I remem-
ber. He has sprung into existence as a powerful youth without
a mother. There is no infancy or childhood to him. He has
simply emerged from the quarry where he was waiting, the
block of marble in which his beauty stood poised, ready, has
fallen from him like the robe a fighter wears.

The gabble of tourists reaches not even to his knees, it is like
dirty water in which someone might have to wade. Indifferent
to enmity and friendship, he turns his head to gaze at the
distance, I will lift up mine eyes unto the hills from whence
cometh my help, *a gesture which reveals the tendon of his neck*
aligned with his thigh, and which he shares with the young
sculptor who habitually without thinking about it glances off
to the side of whomever his body faces be they allies or foes. It is

*not arrogance, exactly. It is a question of work demanding to
be done. Future heroic deeds lie folded in his brain and chest,
packed in his groin, cool whiteness on whiteness, he can feel
them tremble and churn like spirits unborn, like music we can
continue when once we have begun it.*

The Wisdom of Solomon

Wisdom is the principal thing;
therefore get wisdom:
and with all thy getting,
get understanding.
Exalt her, and she shall promote thee:
she shall bring thee to honor
when thou dost embrace her.

PROVERBS 4:7–8

Remember wise old Solomon
Recall his history
He was the wisest man on earth
And so he cursed the day of his birth
He knew that all was vanity.

BERTOLD BRECHT

*I*t is their first meeting, the first day.

They have bathed in cream and been rubbed with myrrh. They have been clothed in bright embroidered silk, sleek fur, sheer wool, fine cotton, and leather more tender than butter. They have adorned themselves in golden and jeweled bracelets, necklaces, rings, noserings, brooches. Their respective crowns rest lightly on their dressed hair. Belladonna causes their eyes to glow. His eyes are large and dark, he is famous for wisdom. She too is famous, her eyes are deep and bright. He is graceful. She is more graceful, black and comely. They have been preparing. Their ambassadors have been in conference, have drawn up papers, have signed papers, have sealed papers.

The musicians play, the choristers sing, the guards stand at attention. Peacocks stroll up and down in the garden, a mother monkey clutching her infant swings to the top of a palmetto and looks down at the queen with human eyes. The minister of protocol nods. Sheba rises. Sheba passes from the garden through cedar doors which close behind her.

She walks toward him lifting her skirts, thinking the palace floor is wet.† But Solomon has made the floor mirrored. There are two of her. He sees the bead of her vulva. You have hairy legs, he says. And you, O king, are growing prematurely bald, she replies. They say, he murmurs, that baldness is a sign of virility. Sheba smiles and lowers her false eyelashes as if abashed. O king, in my country they say a hard man is good to find.

They trade insults mirthfully, they recline on a couch which has been covered in zebra skin for the occasion, they eat some grapes, they smoke some Lebanese hashish. A good thing this is a private audience. I couldn't get much higher, says Solomon. You think not? says Sheba. She takes off her blouse and they discuss botany, one of her special topics. He oils and rubs her back while they discuss jurisprudence, a specialty of his. She rolls over, he pours oil in his palms, he begins massaging her

---

† The story of the glass floor and Solomon's observation about Sheba's legs is a favorite rabbinical tale. Other tales describe Solomon's knowledge of the language of animals, his magical abilities, and even his power over demons.

feet, the triangular pink muscles of sole and heel, the arch, the plump toe cushions and thin alleys between the toes, the crystal ankles. How beautiful are thy feet, oh prince's daughter, he says. Oh, that now is very charming, says the queen. It's mine, he says. The "Song of Songs" is Solomon's. I wrote it this morning in honor of your arrival. Very fine indeed, exclaims Sheba, who as a practical woman is extremely fond of erotic poetry, especially when addressed to herself. I hope you will give me a copy to take home; and please go on.

He recites the "Song of Songs," meanwhile continuing the massage of her legs. Calves, knees, and so forth. A garden shut up, a fountain sealed, is my sister, my bride. His hand touches her crotch. What do you call this in your language, Solomon asks. King Solomon's mines, Sheba replies demurely. She is playing with his interesting circumcised penis about which she has several questions. And now, she says, I must ask you my riddle. She stretches over Solomon in a posture known throughout the fertile crescent as the Sheba position. O king, I have examined your fascinating and unique holy books, perhaps with more attention than your priests. They contain a secret knowledge. Can you tell me what that knowledge is?

Solomon feels himself to be leaping upon the mountains, skipping upon the hills. Concentration is difficult. He tickles Sheba's neck which is like a tower. Alchemy?

No. She licks his left earlobe.

Numerology?

Still less. She bites his right earlobe.

Eschatology? He caresses her warm belly which is like a stack of heaped wheat.

Not in the least; there are no last days; the universe will not go up in flames and rivers of blood, notwithstanding the desire of a few fanatic preachers to see it do so. The arrow of time on which we are flying, to which we are bound, does not simply come to an abrupt halt. In the beginning it is infinitely swift. It gradually decelerates, travels more and more slowly throughout the duration of the universe and finally, gently, by imperceptible degrees, ceases. At this point the velocity of time is zero, entropy is maximal. Nothing will be happening any more, my dear. But life itself will also have gradually ceased, innumerable kalpas earlier. According to some of our sages, the universe remains stable thereafter. A stability of zero significance. According to others, the arrow of time shoots backward, and all events are repeated in reverse, at the end of which entropy has become minimal, and the universe has imploded to the source of time and its condition of pure potential immaterial energy.

Good to know, says Solomon. But what is the secret of holy scripture?

Climb into it and see, says Sheba. Further.

On the second day they have not left the couch. Solomon has told Sheba most of his three thousand parables, each of which has a thousand and five interpretations, and Sheba has told Solomon a fair number of African pygmy jokes. They have eaten swan's eggs, larks' wings, pigeon-brain soup, and rolled breast of ostrich; they have drunk goats' milk, mango juice, and a great quantity of wine. Sheba has got Solomon to roll over, and is examining the archipelago of his vertebrae. Here are some of my country's proverbs, in my own translation, says Sheba.

Sheba's Proverbs

Some people don't have the brain God gave a pigeon.
Dogmatism is a barking hyena caged and fed by Terror.
Paradox is the smile of truth.
Does God reward the virtuous? do frogs love flies?
A confident man is unafraid of an intelligent woman.
An intelligent woman is unafraid of a confident man.
Are you nostalgic for matriarchy? A woman ruler can
    be crueler.
Everyone is afraid; do what you fear.
Whatever doesn't suffer isn't alive.
Exercise benefits the brain.
Laughing and crying lengthen one's life.
Talent is plentiful as blackberries, persistence rarer
    than radium.
How boring the pure male: a language consisting
    of consonants.
How boring the pure female: a language consisting of vowels.
To understand is to laugh; to laugh is to understand.
The fool proposes *either/or*; the wise respond *both/and*.
Truth without lies is like soup without salt.
Truth is a length of cloth embroidered by Beauty. Spread it
    out, fold it in small rectangles, crumple it in your pocket
    and forget it, hang it as a banner, use it to cover the dead;
    for a wedding sheet; and to wrap the newborn child.
Whoever learns a new song is enchanted.

A ruler who cannot feed his people invents a holy war.

Freedom confuses us; absence of freedom destroys us.

Violence in the hand, stupidity in the mind.

Hatred of others is a knife at your own heart.

Tolerance of others is dinner with your mother once a week.

Love of others is the jackpot, the quarter in the slot, the bank
balances pouring over your hands.

Join the army, travel to exotic places, meet interesting new
people and kill them.

Is it right to kill people? No, if they are people. Yes, if they
are the enemy. That is human logic.

Do the rich always abuse the poor? Is the sky blue?

No joy is like the joy when a tyrant falls.

Make trade not war.

Wild women don't worry; wild women don't get the blues.

As desire is desirable, so contempt is contemptible.

Art, like worship, penetrates your space and time.

You catch more flies with honey than vinegar.

Listen to the dead; they are trying to help you.

Some say love is sanity and lust is lunacy; some say the
reverse. What do you say?

The philosopher sits in a desert, and sees that it is a garden.

The mathematician holds a mirror to God.

The poet envies the madman; the painter is the most
cheerful of mortals.

You don't need a weather vane to know which way
the wind blows.

Musicians are honored in heaven.

Damn prisons! Bless playgrounds!

Some of those would be good for bumper stickers, remarks
Solomon. I hoped you would notice, Sheba says. This gives me

an idea for something I might write in middle age, he says. You're so vain, she titters. And that, he says, gives me an idea for something I might write in old age. Vanity of vanities, all is vanity. Do you like that for an opening line?

On the third day Solomon teaches Sheba the language of animals and the language of demons. They stand at a window and listen to a dog bark. Tell me about your life, Sheba says sleepily.

It is not by magic that one acquires an understanding heart, says Solomon. Nor all at once. One must be quick-witted in the first place. In the second place one must be materially comfortable. First feed the face, and then talk right and wrong, as the poet says. It is necessary to read and study for many years. Then it is necessary to travel to numerous cities. It is good to be obsessively hungry for more knowledge than you can attain in a lifetime. It is good, at least once, to have killed somebody, if you want to understand murderers. It is wise to live sometimes among rich men, sometimes among thieves, and sometimes like a bird hopping in the sand.

And then there is the education of your passions. For this it is useful to have someone snap your heart in two pieces like a bread stick. It is important, too, to sit among the mothers in the park, gazing at the babies and smelling their fragrance.

Most important is the cultivation of a sense of guilt. As a youth you should discover that your parents are sinners and hypocrites, and despise them. Your loud tyrannical father so bursting with self-love, your manipulative pretty mother so soft-voiced and seemingly modest, how can you help but hate such people, seeing clearly through them. Then one parent should die, and you should watch the newly dead grow cold, like the streets of a small village in winter. The other should live on, increasingly helpless, with a voice like the mew of a hungry kitten. You should night and day remember the commandment to honor your parents. You should feel their intense eyes on you, and hear their lamenting refrain: We created you, we made you king, we gave you everything, we love you so. . . . You will conclude that you owe to the world the tenderness you were unable to give to your mother and father. It is the same with the other commandments, you cannot keep any of them, yet you want to be virtuous. . . .

Sheba agrees but she is bored. She is not so fond of being lectured to.

And now suppose you believe yourself able to govern a people, the king continues. That is, to govern these Jews. He sits without speaking for a minute, wondering if he ought to tell her, and he thinks: Why not. He shows her all his suffering, lets it come up from his feet to his eyes.

Suppose you establish peace and prosperity. Suppose you have a state in which births outnumber deaths and joys outnumber sorrows. Suppose you support the arts. A free press. Freedom of worship. Free medical care for the poor. A bureaucracy of only moderate corruption. A program of public works. Imagine that farm prices are reasonable. Imagine that by astute diplomacy you have cordial relations with your neighbors. Through your understanding heart, which you cherish above riches and power, you have achieved the happiness of your people. You are a real *mensch,* a good Jew. Incidentally you have riches and power as well, since God is so pleased with you.

Sheba sees which way the wind is blowing now. She puts his head in her lap, she strokes his intelligent damp forehead, she kisses him with the kisses of her mouth.

Suppose you are finally pleased with yourself, says Solomon. Does it matter? When you die, the greedy and stupid will govern as usual. Your son will be a brute and a fool, who will fire his best advisors. Factions will multiply like lice. Your nation will be weak, because people who are happy lose their ferocity. You will be invaded. Your cities will be ashes . . . bare footprints in ashes, donkey trails. . . . And if they build the cities up again they will be destroyed again—blocks knocked over by a clumsy hand. And every time there will be nothing left but sour Jew pain.

In which half of them will believe they are superior to the rest of the world, while the other half will believe they are inferior; or rather, each godforsaken individual of them will be divided on this issue and bleeding at the line of the cut. But they will all believe they are in pain because they are different from other human beings. Different especially from their conquerors. They'll call it being chosen.

Sheba strokes his eyes. From which you conclude? she asks.

From which I conclude, he replies, among other things the following. That all is vanity and a striving after wind. That there is a time and a season for everything. That it is good to eat, drink, and be merry. And that whatsoever my hand findeth to do, I should do it with my might.

Sheba nods and embraces him.

▨

Following three days of conversation interrupted only for showers and room service, King Solomon and the Queen of Sheba have exchanged all their information. Your wives are lucky women, says Sheba. On the contrary, it is I who am lucky, replies Solomon gallantly. I see, says Sheba, that your reputation for wisdom is exceeded only by the fact of it.

He shaves and rings for the steward. Solomon and Sheba proceed ceremonially to the dining room for a farewell banquet, which is to last another three days. Excuse me, says the queen during the hors d'oeuvres. She needs to spend this time in the harem. She has a few things she must discuss with Solomon's seven hundred wives and three hundred concubines.

I would advise you, Sheba says, to permit your wives and concubines to worship the goddesses of their choice upon the high places. To do so will not merely be entertaining for them, it will cause them to be less homesick for their native lands, it will make them believe that they themselves are goddesses which will improve their dispositions, and it will enrich the culture of your country. Perhaps it will improve the crops as well. One never knows.

Of course, says Solomon. I have been waiting for them to ask. What, after all, could better adorn the transcendent unity of the

One God than a plurality of magnificent names, adoring epithets, glorious representations, each expressing a community's fullest imagination of divinity, each a mote of dust in the sandstorm of Creation. God the Father, God the Mother, God the Child, God the Breast-Hill-Mountain, God the Fire, God the Thunder. . . . Consider for example the house I have created for the Holy One who is the God of my fathers. There it is, a hollow bit of carved timber and stones standing on its inconsequential mountain: a container for the almighty. A spice box for sweet things. I understand the need for such buildings, I understand their irony. Like all symbols it faces two ways. A lie, a truth.

Is the God of my fathers a lie, a truth, an absurdity? I built the temple because my father wanted me to. The work required thirty thousand men and took seven years. Inside, the walls, floor, and ceiling are entirely covered with pure gold, carved into cherubim, palm trees, and open flowers, and garnished with precious jewels. It contains a brass altar standing on twelve oxen, brass vessels and instruments, golden candlesticks, and a veiled tabernacle into which God is presumed to enter. The building is a tremendous popular success, severe in design to express the exaltedness of our god, but on the other hand quite costly in order to express his glory. When it was finished I prayed aloud to the Divine One, declaring what I obviously already knew. *Behold, the heaven of heavens cannot contain thee; how much less this house that I have builded.* Yet if the people believe that God inhabits the temple, they are correct. Can you guess the answer to this riddle?

Yes, says Sheba. What a sweet man, she thinks.

Finally her camels are saddled, her carloads of gifts packed, her retinue recovered from the festivities. Guards stand at attention in the king's courtyard, the sun has risen above the trans-Jordan hills, it is a cool winter morning. In the Red Sea her ship is waiting. Goodbye, my dear, she says, shaking Solomon's hand. It has been a most wonderful summit. She kisses him on both cheeks in the Oriental fashion, enjoying the brisk texture of his beard as he enjoys the electrical charge of her lips, their perfumes combine in the air, they both breathe deeply and sigh. Please write, says Solomon. Yes, says Sheba.

Though She Delay

The Return of the Mothers

Esther, or the World
Turned Upside Down

*And the letters were sent by posts into all the
king's provinces, to destroy, to kill, and to cause to
perish, all Jews, both young and old, little
children and women.*
THE BOOK OF ESTHER, 3:13.

So many Hamans, and just one Purim.
JEWISH PROVERB

They tell the story of Esther to children. It's a folk tale. Horror wrapped up as entertainment, threat of annihilation averted. Once a year we imagine the victory of the powerless as a game. Casting lots? Take a chance on Mordecai. And watch those plot twists. Number One Wife Vashti demoted for discipline problems. Esther wins Miss Persia contest to replace her. Sexy Jewess announces If I perish, I perish, and reveals secret of birth. Beauty queen becomes savior of her people. Evil scheme foiled, wicked Haman impaled on his own scaffold. A poke at the principalities and powers. King Ahasuerus, drunk again, countermands earlier order to kill all Jews. In a startling reverse move, all Jews get to kill their enemies.

The story is good for thousands of years, for we have scrolled forward in history, into the normal life of empires where helpless people are crushed as a matter of course, and divine intervention is in permanent recess. Already it is evident that the Jews, a people proudly apart, are available as scapegoats to the mighty and the many, that the malice of human beings will find us especially delectable. We differ. We do not bow down to gods other than our own. That is reason enough for them to hate us and want us destroyed.

Naturally we celebrate this one day of deliverance, in which everything is turned upside down, by feasting and merrymaking. The buds are bursting on the trees, birds stitch across the earth to mate and nest build, the conventionalities of hope assume physical reality among the juices of spring. There is a time for hilarity. Sticky sap flows. Children don costumes. Men and women disguise themselves in each other's clothing, which is otherwise forbidden. When the story is retold, everyone present yells, hoots and rattles a noisemaker each time the name of Haman is mentioned. The saying also goes that one should drink, on Purim, until one cannot tell good from evil, blessed be Mordecai from cursed be Haman.

☒

Mordecai changes Esther's life, introduces her to her Jewish identity. In a similar way my grandfather changes me. I am in his lap getting close to the smells of pipe tobacco and wool, enthroned where so often I have heard him tell the Story of the Man Who Travelled from Place to Place. I am his shayne maydele, his pretty little girl, his one grandchild. He gives me Life Savers on the sly, he glows at me through his glasses, he makes me show how I can already read, he is teaching me to play checkers.

*It is Saturday. All week I have been in Kindergarten. We
learned right away to salute the Flag, now we are learning
about democracy and elections. I ask my grandfather who he
will vote for in the next election, knowing that he will say
Roosevelt, since everyone I know will vote for Roosevelt, so we
can finish beating Hitler and the Japs. I rub my cheek
against his scratchy cardigan. He says nothing. Then he says
he is not going to vote. I am shocked. I sit up tall in his lap to
give him a lesson about democracy. My grandfather's arms
are around me but he looks away, something changes in the
air. For a moment I believe I have won the argument, then he
says that he will not vote for any president because no president will save the Jews in Europe. It is the first time I have
heard that phrase: the Jews in Europe.*

*A quarter century later my mother describes a game they had
when she was a young girl. She would come into the house and
rush at her father with her arms wide, laughing, as if to
embrace him; he would run around the apartment, around
the furniture, as if he were afraid. She would chase after him
and he would yell Oy! Oy! mih shlugte di Yidn! Help, help,
they're killing the Jews.*

*A quarter century later my husband repeats what his father
told him and his brothers: In the old country, you would be
soap now.*

*It would be false to say that I am being shoved forward in a
line of human skeletons outside the city of Kiev, embracing to
my chest a book of poetry which, although I am only five, I can
already read. False to say that I am huddled in a sewer under
the city of Warsaw frowning over a map. I am not in the*

woods checking a rifle. No, it is a Saturday afternoon in
September 1944 in Borough Park, Brooklyn, America. I am
the most ignorant possible American child in my pinafore,
sitting on the knees of my Socialist grandfather just outside
the kitchen where my mother and grandmother drink hot tea
in glasses, the sugar settled in a sweet dissolving heap at the
bottom. It would be correct to say that the air around me has
changed, has acquired a greater transparency. It is like stories
of time travel, where you find yourself unwarned in some
alternative universe with new laws of physics. I have no idea
what my grandfather means. At the same time, I understand
perfectly. I have instantly acquired awareness of a global grief.

An initiation, a kindness without walls, a bitterness without
floor—the familiar Brooklyn apartment seems for that
instant to have dissolved—an instant and permanent canker
on a child's budding patriotism. He squeezes my shoulder, the
terrible danger that he will cry is past, I jump from his lap
and go in the kitchen for tea. Now I understand that inside is
always different from outside, reality from appearance, depth
from surface. Don't expect me to forget.

🖾

Orphan: she learns to read. She learns to write. She is a pretty
girl. She is a beautiful woman. She has grown up in the penumbra of her cousin's ambitions, which inhabit the air around him
like furious red sparks zigzagging from an invisible bonfire,
when he is calculating, making plans. At times when he suffers
disappointment, it is as if a fleet of swallows careened madly
around him, wailing, their wings and tails pointed as darts.
When angry, he is stubborn as a bull. There are enemies, he
says, everywhere. Around her, however, the aura remains glit-

tering, serene, protective. She is an undemanding woman. And her parents, and theirs, and the past? Nothing, nowhere, all of that, the past, belongs to Mordecai. Esther is a pretty girl, a beautiful woman, to whom everything is pleasing. Like a dream, like the glow of dawn in which pulses the spark of a lonely star. She is a Jew. She is not a Jew.

A royal interlude. In the palace, Vashti has refused to appear when summoned, to display herself to the feasting princes. Too proud for her own good, a dangerous example, rumors ripple through the capital, and out into the woods and hills and throughout the kingdom. For this deed of the queen will come abroad unto all women, to make their husbands contemptible in their eyes. At the center of the ripples, however, the water has become smooth. The marble palace, like a block of ice, has promulgated an edict written in the king's name and sealed with the king's ring, that all wives should honor their husbands, both great and small. The wives smile narrowly, and look with narrow amusement from the corners of their eyes, and the queen has disappeared, leaving smooth water.

Like the glow of dawn in which a lonely star radiates, Esther is surely a beautiful woman. She is the most beautiful woman in Persia. She is a queen. She has the breasts of a queen, like honeydew melons. She has the knees of a queen, like crystal. She has the hair of a queen. She has the red fingernails of a queen, like poppies. She has the scent of a queen. She is a Jew. She is not a Jew. She behaves like a tame animal, a large gilded carp swimming most gracefully and languidly among the fishes of the women's aquarium, the harem. Once an orphan, today Esther wears on her head the royal crown, or turban, or scroll, or megillah, as the king has placed it. Ah, but she can read and write. He made her learn, the clever cousin. Not every queen can read and write. And he walks every day outside the court of the women's house, to find out how she is, and what will become of her. In his opinion, enemies are everywhere.

▨

The party is in full swing. Sequins and cigars. Numerous uncles and aunts, great-uncles, grand-aunts, cousins thrice removed, in-law women and their toddlers, a hurricane of family carrying who knows how many branches with it, sweeps tumultuously past me, celebrating its annual survival. My twig of family being the poor relations invited once or twice a year, I don't know these people but I watch them. The bosoms of the women heave, their ample hips undulate, in turquoise taffeta and yellow-and-black ruffled silk, their stockings with black seams down the calves heading for the buffet.

A groaning buffet of food. Chopped chicken livers with schmaltz, gefilte fish, potato latkes, pot roast, celery, beets, gleaming fats. Enormous challah from which to rip pieces, hamantashen like a small Mount Sinai. Eat, my child, eat. The very walls murmuring eat, my darling, eat. The cheek-kissing followed by rubbing lipstick off the cheek, waves of scent lapping the room, the aunts talk about furs, marriages, illnesses, the children going to college, law school, medical school, reprieve, safety. The male bandying, the brandy they are allowing the children to taste, the gossipy shrieking, the men talk garment district, talk lawyers, deals, racetrack, and the brains of their sons.

Some uncles collect like minnows around a big fish up from

*Washington. A fat uncle standing on a kitchen chair takes
flashbulb pictures mainly of his own three fat daughters, tie
loosened, big shoulders, pushes people aside, saying Just one
minute, excuse me. Children throwing nuts and raisins, small
children already whining and tugging on their mothers. The
teenage cousins playing with the dreidels and flirting. Everyone eats as if attempting to fill the bellies of the starved, the
long dead, they make noise as if to penetrate the ears of the six
million. We've escaped, they are shouting. Look at us, we are
alive! We're in one piece!*

*If the six million could see my family, if they could see all the
families coagulated together like balls of food, would they
rejoice? Would they be reassured, would they weep?*

They say her clever cousin is in sackcloth, bitterly mourning.
Word comes to the queen. The queen sends word, why. The
messenger hurries from the grate of an outer courtyard, through
secret doors and secret corridors. Men in uniform bow and
recede, like potted ferns waving in a wind. The message is that
Haman the Agagite, descendant of the Amalekites, has written
an edict in the king's name and sealed it with the king's ring, to
destroy, to slay, and to cause to perish, all Jews, both young and
old, little children and women, in one day. Now Mordecai the
Jew, descendant of Saul the Benjamite, wishes her to save the
people.

They say the capital is in an uproar, because it is full of Jews.
They cannot wish to kill her, she is beautiful, she is the most

beautiful woman in Persia, she is the queen. Tell him, she says, I am afraid. Tell him I cannot help, tell him I am only a woman. A fish. She floats away, flirting her transparent tail mournfully.

I wish to be invisible. I am invisible. Retracted as a snail, I wander along the walls looking at family photographs in gilt frames. If I play dreidels I always lose because my cousins cheat. If I sit in a chair by myself they'll tell me to go enjoy the party. If I flee to the toilet and stay in there reading a magazine a great-aunt will knock, she'll ask am I sick, do I have a fever, a stomach ache, what's the matter, a hand to my brow, her perfume suffocating me. My impulse is to steal to the bedroom where the coats are, fling myself on the pile, crawl in among them. No, I am not Queen Esther, nor was meant to be. Am a bookish adolescent who cannot imagine how anyone can admire those sickening feminine wiles. Am rebel Vashti, too proud to obey that loutish king. The whole story infuriates me, especially the part about touching the tip of the king's sceptre, how crude can you get. And why can't they understand that I really want to save my people, save humanity. A lot they care. A lot Esther herself cared, the selfish thing, Mordecai had to tell her she'd be killed with the rest of her people, before she was willing to lift a finger. That doll, that puppet.

She is a Jew. She is. Yes, she is a Jew, she instructs herself, ashamed, afraid, ready. Sweating through her perfume, shivering in her royal garments. Cedar doors, secret corridors. From her warm inner room to the court, doing exactly what she fears, breaking the law, there she goes. Nobody has called her. She has to do it, walk on her hobbled legs, speak with her throttled voice. To the one who wants to kill her she must be charming. She must make her voice musical and issue an invitation.

She instructs herself not to laugh, not to scream, not to spit in his face, not seize the sceptre from his hand and strike him with it, not to throw up out of pure cold terror. To act, to control her body, to be lovely, to be merry. She rehearses. If I please the king, and if I have found favor in his sight, and the thing seem right before the king, and I be pleasing in his eyes.

Her predecessor refused, she must not refuse. Her body needs to undo the king's writing, scatter the letters, break the royal seal that they say is unbreakable, retract the royal edict they say is changeless. Does she stand on the shoulders of the old queen, does the dead one encourage her?

Obviously he may kill her. She is breaking and entering. Chilly, lofty, empty, the place of power. Its vacuum streaked with gold, the pavement of green, and white, and shell, and onyx marble, and at its furthest end a throne. She feels as if the throne is infinitely distant. I am a Jew, she instructs herself, willing a blush of beauty onto her cheeks, a pout of pleasure onto her lips. Take a deep breath, magnify the breasts. I will do what I fear. And if I perish, I perish.

 The big fish from Washington touches glasses with my prettiest cousin. She flashes her eyes, tosses her auburn mane. My snail self peers forth at them. Years later I will

think: we save ourselves as best we can, we use whatever we have. Beauty, friends in high places, a rifle in the woods with the partisans, a fountain pen, whatever works. No, I am not ready to think this way. I am not ready to wonder if Vashti and Esther could be secret allies, ridicule of the king joined to manipulation of the king. Sleek small moles under the ground of tyranny, grain by grain overturning the world. I am thinking how my cousin is beautiful, I am clumsy, she catches men in her net while I crawl sullenly along the wall's base-board leaving my snail trail.

Who are my enemies, who are my allies, how do I learn to recognize them. In the settlement house camp when I was a junior counselor, the senior counselor was a freckle-faced Irishwoman who made everybody laugh. The kids in our fourth-grade bunk loved her, so did I. She was strict but she made up for it by being funny. She would make us roll with laughter at her jokes. All summer, though I tried and failed to please her, I continued to think she was wonderful. When I would tell the kids to do something and she would command them to do something else, I felt ashamed of my failure.

The last week of camp I was in charge one rest hour. My senior counselor's daughter bounced on her bed, acting up. She was a child with blond curly hair and angelic looks but a less than angelic temperament. I told her to be quiet. She kept bounc-ing. I told her again and she bounced higher. I said she knew what the rules were and she should have some consideration for others. Suddenly the child's peachlike complexion turned beet red and she shook with anger. I don't have to obey you, she shouted at me. I'm a Catholic! Oh, I thought—as the summer

interpreted itself—so that was why. Now I watch the big fish
say something to my pretty cousin, who puts her hand over her
mouth, red fingernails, laughing prettily. Pretending to
laugh. She leans back, scans the room, merry eyes, sees me. I
am invisible, a snail, but she sees me, winks at me. And now
the uncles and aunts are mostly drunk, draped over one
another's shoulders, what cacophony, the exhibitionist ones
dance, stamp their feet, kick into the air, circling ferociously,
unwilling ever to surrender their sexuality, festive to the point
of blindness, alive, alive.

So there's the whole story, the gantze megillah, the happy
ending. Doesn't that crown everything? Scroll forward. Let's
have a drink. But the story is not the story. The beginning is not
the beginning. Repeat it. Before words, our bodies. My body. I
trick him, I fool him, I make him drunk, I unwrite the writing.
Ever-returning spring. When I remember myself. When times
fly backward, forward, when I/we make him dizzy with desire.
When we punish our enemies. This festival has been celebrated
forever. Man and woman doubled, the slayer slain, and a tree
growing upside down. So who do we think we are? Hadassah
the myrtle tree with her flowers like stars. Esther who is Ishtar
(Ashtaroth, Astarte, locked out the door, creeps in the window), morning and evening star. Lady of battles, opener of the
womb, forgiver of sins. Ishtar whose song is sweeter than honey and wine, sweeter than sprouts and herbs, superior even to
pure cream. Ishtar whom Gilgamesh accuses of slaying her
lovers. Half laughter, half killer. Coupled with Mordecai,
Marduk, bull calf of the sun, armed and winged. Babylonian

Ishtar and Marduk having destroyed their enemies, just like that, a new year destroys the old.[†] Let's leaf. This festival has been calibrated forever. Fast-forward, fast-backward. Put on your mask and dance.

I am and am not a Jew. We are and are not Babylonian, Assyrian, Canaanite. She is and is not the court favorite, the assimilated one, the hidden Marronite, the soul in exile, the weeping Shekhinah. We disguise our bodies. Our old bodies. Like truth budding from lies. Our ever-returning bodies. Dying and being born. Overturning the world.

[†] *The Golden Bough* relates Purim to the Babylonian spring festival of Zagmuk, in which the *Enuma Elish* (of which Marduk is the hero) was recited, and the king renewed his power by grasping the hands of Marduk in the temple; and to the Saceaen Saturnalia in which a condemned prisoner was allowed to play king, making free with the king's courtesans, then executed. Ishtar, a goddess of both sexuality and war, in part derived from the Sumerian Innanna, was worshipped throughout the Near East. Vashti and Haman were an Elamite divine pair, according to Patricia Monaghan, *The Book of Goddesses and Heroines.* Scrolling forward, *The Encyclopedia of Religion* (ed. Mircea Eliade) observes that Esther in the Middle Ages was identified with the court Jew who risked everything to support fellow-Jews; was a favorite of the Spanish Marronites who saw her disguise as symbolic of their own; and was even at times identified with the Shekhinah, as the absence of God in the Scroll of Esther symbolized the hiddenness of the Shekhinah in the world and in exile.

Job, or a
Meditation on Justice

Though he slay me, yet will I trust in him. . . .
And though after this skin worms destroy my body,
yet in my flesh I shall see God. Whom I shall see
for myself, and mine eye shall behold, and not
another, though my reins be consumed within me.

JOB 13:15, 19:20–21

Blessed art thou, No-one.
For thy sake we
will bloom.
Towards
thee.

PAUL CELAN

*I*t is a cold, rainy November evening. The rain began in
the afternoon. I walk home from the bus without an
umbrella, hunched under the downpour, and strip off my
soaked things; I get a robe on, wrap a towel around my head,
start heating up some leftover stew, and settle at the kitchen
table. Nobody else is home. My two daughters are at college in
Boston. My husband is at a meeting in Chicago. My son, still
in high school, is at his karate lesson. Mail is strewn across the
kitchen, where I left it this morning, along with the morning's
New York Times, *the day's poverty fattened by the day's*
advertisements. The customary cognitive dissonance, the

*mothers of Chilean desaparecidos, holding photographs of their
missing and by now probably tortured or killed children,
embraced by a pre-Thanksgiving fur sale. I have a stack of
student papers to read. For no apparent reason I pick up a
notebook and begin to jot down some thoughts about the Book
of Job and the idea of justice.*

It is a strange invention of the children of God, God's justice.
That God should be just, obliged to reward good men who
obeyed his laws, cared for widows and the poor and so forth,
and punish evil ones who did not, was not a notion that occurred to the Egyptians, the Canaanites, the Babylonians, the
Greeks. We should appreciate, if we step back from our theological assumptions, what a peculiar expectation it is that human justice should be intrinsic to a God, and still more odd,
that human beings need to remind the god about it, as Abraham
does before the destruction of Sodom, and as Job does when he
complains of his afflictions. They remind God that he is not
supposed to harm the guiltless.

In the simple folktale frame to the story of Job, from whose
center sublime poetry will explode, the tone is matter of fact. It
is business as usual. God and Satan converse one day in heaven,
God points out his servant Job, Satan remarks that Job's love of
God has never been tested by suffering, so God gives Satan
permission to afflict Job. First Job's cattle are killed, then his
children, and finally his body is afflicted with unbearable boils.
Job is at first patient, then his patience breaks down, he demands an explanation.

Here the poetry erupts. It erupts from agony, puncturing the

surface of the text and pouring forth like lava, like the boils that
have ruptured Job's skin, like an interior sickness. His abused
body not merely speaks but wails, in an effort to make itself
heard. The sufferer curses his birth, confesses God's absolute
power over him, and desires to die. His friends who have gathered to comfort him are shocked. Despair is an act of blasphe-
my. Yet Job sits naked upon his ash heap and despairs.

Now when Job confronts God of course God is not put exactly
in the wrong. But there is challenge and debate. The friends
insist that Job must have secretly sinned or he wouldn't be
suffering, and that no mortal has the right to question God. Job,
scraping his scabs, denies any wrongdoing. Goaded by his
body's experience of pain, his knowledge of the world's pain,
the remorseless remoteness of this being who evidently exter-
minates both honest and wicked, and the piety of these sancti-
monious friends, he calls God to account. *Though he slay me,
yet will I trust in him; but I will maintain my own ways before him.*
Silence. The silence of God. Job is like poor mad Saul, abandoned by God, but unlike Saul, he contests his abandonment.
He hungers for presence and not absence. He demands law and
justice instead of accident and chaos.† *Oh that I knew where I
might find him! that I might come even to his seat! I would order
my cause before him, and fill my mouth with arguments.*

---

† Impossible not to quote Buber on the Book of Job. "Instead of his God,
for whom he looks in vain, his God, who had not only put sufferings upon
him but had also 'hedged him in' until 'His way was hid' from his eyes
(3:23), there now came and visited him on his ash heap *religion,* which uses
every act of speech to take away from him the God of his soul. Instead of the
'cruel' and living God, to whom he clings, religion offers him a reasonable
and rational God, a deity whom he, Job, does not perceive either in his own
existence or in the world, and who obviously is not to be found anywhere
save only in the very domain of religion."

When the Lord answers Job out of the whirlwind—*Who is this that darkeneth counsel by words without knowledge?*—his magnificent speech seems designed to smash Job and mankind into humility by an overwhelming display of creative might. Where the anguish of Job is volcanic, the mockery of God is cosmic. Were you there when I created the earth, the morning stars that sang together, the floods, behemoth, leviathan, the horse that has a neck clothed with thunder and saith among the trumpets, Ha ha? Is it you who guides Arcturus, is it you who gives the eagle the taste for blood? Have you an arm like God? I am the Creator! I am the Destroyer! I am not just! I have nothing to do with justice![†]—That is the essence of the Lord's reply, and it is very splendid to read, the verbal equivalent of a thermonuclear explosion.

Job repents in dust and ashes. The poem closes there. And yet the very end of the Book of Job, the folktale frame of the story where Job gets everything back and is richer than before, evidently vindicates man and his challenge and is almost a divine apology. It is as if God were saying: It's true that I'm unjust and that's the way I like it, and of course the conventional religion of your friends that claims that I am just and that your suffering is justified is false as you are well aware; but, do you know, you have embarrassed me a little. There. I hereby rebuke your friends and give you back your health, sons, daughters, and

---

[†] Stephen Mitchell, in the introduction to his translation of the Book of Job, notes the cosmic humor of the Voice from the whirlwind, and compares it to Krishna's response to Arjuna in the Baghavad-Gita, "in which that prince experiences, down to the marrow of his bones, the glory and the terror of the universe, all creation and all destruction, embraced in the blissful play of the Supreme Lord."

cattle. And Job was more blessed in his latter end than his beginning, they will repeat. For it is important that reputation, too, be repaired.

No woman can read the story without thinking: other sons, other daughters, other cattle. Not the original ones, who were killed when enemies attacked, when the fire fell from heaven, and when the great wind instantly destroyed her eldest son's house while all her children were eating and drinking there. The dead ones are permanently dead. The daughter who could run as fast as a boy, the one with the sharp temper. The gentle one with the eyes of a deer. The son who was wild and lazy, along with the secret, sententious, prosperous and hard-working one. They are under the ground now, seven sons, three daughters. Anyone can walk back and forth on top of them, and they do nothing. *I only am escaped alone to tell thee,* said each servant after each malefic catastrophe, a sentence she well remembers. Job has his recompense but the killed children remain under the ground where she cannot touch them again.

And by the way, who compensates the wife, who has had to live with Job in all his phases: as righteous and complacent servant of God and super-holy man; as stricken beast; as the vibrant rhapsodist of an absent justice? She would be cooking mutton stew and mending shirts. He in all his phases the focus of the story, she occupies its periphery, like the sheep and the sons and daughters, but preserved alive so that she can be conscious of her peripheral status, rather than mercifully and suddenly annihilated. Job has many lines to say in the Book of Job but Job's wife has one line and says it early: *Curse God and die.* That is woman's wisdom. Look at it, a large cinder in her outstretched palm.

For she knows all along that God is not just. Never in her heart of hearts has she been deluded by the pieties she mouths along with the rest of the community. Any fool who looks with her eyes can see that God is not just—to daughters, to wives, to mothers. They don't even exist for him. As for the man's world, why do the wicked prosper? Is that not a reasonable question? But her husband has been lucky, and naively believes his good fortune is the consequence of his uprightness. So when he is stricken, and complains, she rushes in immediately with her knowledge, of which the distillation is "curse God and die." It is interesting that he has to do this, in her eyes; perform this brave rebellion; for her, too, he is the protagonist. A husband is a sort of dinosaur, large and clumsy, bellowing when wounded. The wife feels herself to be like a green lizard, slipping among the pebbles between his feet. She could never curse God and die herself. Shrew that she is, she is too timid for heroism.

I understand that because I too, shrew that I am, am shy, lizard-like, not yet angered enough. I who am wife and mother, like the nameless wife of Job. Like most women everywhere and at all times. We mutter if they kill our children. If they throw our men down mine shafts, into armies, onto the garbage dumps of cities, we mourn. Look at us, materialized on the nightly news, swathed in our uniform black, keening and striking our breasts. Look at us in the famous prize-winning photographs. As Edgar Allen Poe said the most poetical subject was the death of a beautiful woman, so the most journalistic subject is female grief over the death of our young in wartime, famine, tyranny. Afterward we return to our assigned tasks of birth and nurture, believing ourselves impotent to protest. We permit life, the jewel in our outstretched hand, to become a cinder.

When my mother was born, the doctor told her mother to let her die. She was a runt, barely four pounds, her spastic stomach couldn't hold food down, she threw everything up immediately. Her mother had neither money nor milk. Have another child when you can afford to eat yourself, said the doctor. My grandmother rigged up an incubator in her bedroom with lamps and pots of steaming water. When my mother threw up she fed her again; and then again. It took six months for my mother's body to learn to hold its food.

When my mother gave birth to me, she refused medication. Then she told the hospital staff she planned to breast-feed me. They replied that this was unsanitary and primitive. They showed her how to make formula, the modern method of feeding infants. When she insisted on breast-feeding they all laughed. You'll put that child on a bottle soon enough when you get home, they said. A month later she took the subway back to the hospital, took the stairs two at a time to the maternity ward, and showed the nurses how a woman suckles a one-month child.

During my first pregnancy I found myself thinking of the war that had been finished in my childhood, and the millions of people incinerated by it. The ovens in the camps, the fire-bombing of Dresden, the destruction of Hiroshima and Nagasaki came vividly to life. I felt an absurd responsibility and would wake up at night confused. I tried to convince myself: the only thing one can do for the dead is to bring new life into the world. In a poem, I wrote: Whoever has died, I make this child for you. After my daughter's birth, I used to enjoy night feedings when I could listen to the creak of my rocking chair and the click of her sucking tongue against her palate while she nursed. I liked the silence surrounding the bedroom. One night, for the space of five or ten minutes perhaps, I sensed the simultaneous presence of every living being on the planet. The air was transparent again, as it was for a few moments when I was five, on my grandfather's lap. This time I felt empowered to feed them all. To feed them love. They were mine, mine. Connected to me and to one another. That was the message in the milk, and whether it was I transmitting this message to my infant daughter, or she transmitting it to me, I could not tell. I wanted to retain it, that blissful awareness. Of course it dissipated, departed, just as the children themselves, in growing, grow estranged.

Today I think: without rage, love is helpless. We are not yet angry enough. Not yet bitter enough. I look at the paper with its headlines as black as vultures and its old bad news. The disappeared, like ghosts of the shine on their rulers' boots. My bread tastes like sand. I finish my coffee and try to forget what I know. The woman of whom we are portions has not yet demanded justice.

🔲

But one day it will be the woman who rises, wounded and agonized, empty-handed, having thrown away needle and kettle, her body pustulant from crown to toes. Rage will blister her and the blisters will be bursting as it were an orchestra playing. Tiny as her body is, insignificant speck as she knows herself to be in God's universe, she will become so swollen with her demand—justice for me! Justice for me!—that she will bellow it out against all rationality. And when she makes that cry, God will appear violently to her and the play will be played. What happened to her husband Job will now happen to her. She will taste, bitterly on her tongue, the condensed cruelty and beauty of the universe. She will recognize her own nothingness as she has never done before, and the experience will be the most rapturous torment for her so that she wishes only to be dead and not conscious, or crazy and not conscious, and she fears she will be made to stay alive forever with this consciousness unchanged, bright as a thousand suns. That would indeed be hell. She repents in dust and ashes. And then finally God will recompense her. It will have to be a large recompense. God will be embarrassed by her as by her husband Job.

Or rather, he was waiting for her to issue her challenge. That is what really happens. God does not know how to be just until the children demand it. Then he knows. Then he responds. After all, he is merely the laws of physics, the magnificent laws of physics, and then the adorable laws of biology. And finally, circuit by ticking circuit through the neural nets, the exquisite laws of conscience.[†]

[†] The two conclusions of the Book of Job are like the two versions of creation, the two versions of David's advent, and other pieces of biblical stitchery. Just at the stretched seam—where light pierces the seam?— we experience God's paradoxical essence as the One of whom all contraries are equally true, or as the binding energy that holds together what would otherwise fly apart. "I form the light, and create darkness: I make peace, and create evil: I the Lord do all these things" (Isaiah 45:7). For the rich tradition of Jewish writers who challenge God, see Josephine Zadovsky Knopp, *The Trial of Judaism in Contemporary Jewish Writing,* and Anson Laytner, *Arguing with God.* Within this tradition, fed perhaps by Lurianic Kabbalism

So she will need a large recompense because she will be asking: Where are my dead sons? What about the women executed as witches and whores? What of the beaten wives? What of the massacred Sioux, the deliberately starved Ukrainians? Why do the bones of many million Africans lie rotting below the Atlantic Ocean? Where are the souls who rose in smoke over Auschwitz? You teach me to say *The wicked shall vanish like smoke, when all tyranny shall be removed from the earth,* but it was innocent babies who vanished. She wants the unjustly slain to be alive and for singing and dance to come to the victims. Somewhere in her reptile brain she hopes the Lord will run the film backward, so that she can see, speedily in her time, the smoke coagulate and pour back down the chimneys, the stream of naked Jews Gypsies Poles partisans homosexuals grandfathers and schoolchildren walk backward out of the buildings, still alive.

We already know what she wants. She wants justice to rain down like waters. She wants adjustment, portion to portion, so that the machinery of the world will look seemly and move powerfully and not scrape and scream. The children of God do not really say that God is just. But they invent the idea. They chew it over and over, holding it up to the light this way and that. And though blood drips from the concept, staining their hands, they are persistent. It is their idea. They want justice to rain down like waters. Justice to rain like waters. Justice to rain. Justice to rain.

---

with its faith in a God conceived as dynamic rather than static, lies the germ of a God whose essence may be transformed through human acts of goodness.

Tree of Life

She is a tree of life to them that lay hold upon her:
and happy is every one who retaineth her.
PROVERBS 3:18

Why did I want the gift of prophecy, come what
may? To speak with my voice; the ultimate.
CHRISTA WOLF

*M*y friend telephones. Her mother died a year ago, they
are choosing a stone, the family expects her to produce
a text. Well, I say, what about Proverbs. Who can find a
virtuous woman? Her price is above rubies. She openeth her
mouth with wisdom. She looketh well to the ways of her household, etcetera.

*I am so fed up with that, growls my friend. It fits all too well.
Is there nothing else one can say about one's mother? There
must be some biblical women who do something besides being
housewives.*

It is true that the women increase and multiply as the texts grow
more modern. There is Huldah the prophetess dwelling in the

college of Jerusalem to whom Josiah sends to explain the scroll (probably proto-Deuteronomy) found in the ruins of the temple by the workmen repairing it. We are not told why he sends to Huldah instead of her contemporary Jeremiah, but she correctly predicts the fall of Judah. There is Judith the voluptuous widow who beheads the besieging Assyrian general Holofernes with his own sword in his tent, thereby saving her city. Huldah and Judith are somehow not in demand at present. There is Susannah, the young beauty unjustly accused of adultery by the lecherous elders whose advances she has rejected. Since women cannot be witnesses in trials, she cannot plead in her own defense, cannot take back the night, the afternoon, or anything. About to be executed, she is saved by the young Daniel. Not a useful model today. There are the two types of women represented in Proverbs: the harlot who draws the young man's feet to hell, and the virtuous wife, whom we have met before. And then there is Wisdom, hochmah, who played smiling in God's face before the creation of the world, whose price is above rubies, and who is a tree of life to them that lay hold on her.

I think of God, as the prophets tell us, being fed up with fat of lambs, sick of new moons and feasts, hating and despising ritual, demanding instead that people care for widows and orphans and stop grinding the faces of the poor. I think of God wanting to see some social action. I wonder if Wisdom is fed up with the price above rubies and enjoys seeing females leave the house, slam the door, get elected to Congress, become doctors lawyers judges artists writers architects musicians scientists mathematicians warriors.

Wisdom who is and is not the virtuous wife, who is and is not the Shekhinah.[†]

She who is God's Dwelling or Presence on earth, or feminine aspect, or tenth kabbalistic sephirah, who in Abraham's time inhabited Sarah, in Isaac's time Rebecca, in Jacob's time Rachel. She who when the temple fell, accompanied Israel into exile. It is also said that she remains hovering at the Western Wall, among the pigeons, to welcome whoever returns. It is said that she mourns, and spreads her wings to comfort the afflicted. If two sit together and the words between them are of Torah, it is said that the Shekhinah is in their midst. In addition, it is said that loving peace and pursuing peace is equal to all the commandments of Torah, and that one should love mankind and lead them under the wings of the Shekhinah. It is said that she seeks the beloved One from whom she has been divided since

---

[†] The mysterious figure of Huldah is in II Kings 23. The midrash says that she was a kinswoman of Jeremiah and that they conducted an academy together, he preaching to the men, she to the women. The Book of Judith and the Story of Susannah are in the Apocrypha. Wisdom, the central allegorical figure of the Book of Proverbs, is a personified abstraction at times represented as God's companion before and during creation (Proverbs 8); at times like the mistress of a noble house (Proverbs 9). In the Apocryphal Wisdom of Solomon she is both an emanation of God and the bride of the wise man. In seeing Wisdom as homologous to the Shekhinah, who is non-biblical but appears in Talmud and Kabbalah, I follow Raphael Patai and Gershom Scholem. What these two female figures (or figures of speech) have in common is that they mediate abundantly between transcendence and immanence, the world of the divine and the world of daily life, eternity and the here and now. They are both severe and generous, they are both active and alive—and both have inspired intense devotion, longing, and desire.

the moment of creation. It is said that the performance of mitzvot, good deeds, works toward their holy reunion and sacred remarriage, and that when a man and his wife make love on the sabbath it is specially propitious.

I wonder if she enters the bodies of prostitutes and cancer victims. I wonder if she is in the breasts of lesbian lovers and video producers, in the rusty knuckles of homeless ladies, in the thin knees and ankles of salesgirls. I wonder if her sorrow is like our sorrow. And how long, how many centuries we must wait.

> Where are the women through whom the Shekhinah
> Will come, will reveal herself, will act
> Will decide to speak
>
> Will command to speak

My friend is a working woman. She leads a busy life and has very little patience for metaphysical speculation. So far as she is concerned, whether there is a God or there is not a God, a Shekhinah or not a Shekhinah, you still have to fight City Hall. The Administration. The Pentagon. she has a meeting to go to. She reminds me of my mother-in-law. When I suggest that she could use the tree of life quote for her mother's stone, she says she will think about it.

Intensive Care

One generation passeth away, another generation
cometh: but the earth abideth for ever.
ECCLESIASTES 1:4

The whole earth is our hospital.
T. S. ELIOT

You seem to be having trouble breathing. He shakes his
head. No. The reporter pursues. Do you have a statement
to make about your condition? The television cameras incline,
like attentive sympathetic intimate friends, a shade more near,
cocking their heads and making whirring noises. There is a
crowd; and each network is said to command billions of view-
ers daily thanks to simultaneous translation in two thousand
indigenous languages, a triumph of contemporary linguistic
technology. Like a drummer tapping out a cadenza high as a
Japanese kite, flashbulbs are popping: like Argentinean dande-
lions, wild and rapid and energetic.

Every camera an insect king. Bloodsuckers, he thinks, since his
mind naturally runs toward analogy and there is no reason for
it to pause now, the pain neither concerns nor confuses his
mind. An image is like tasty blood to them; or like a whiff of
something nice; for it has been demonstrated by experiments
with crushed glands that pheronomes for the bug kingdom are
both the neon and the movie. I am the refuge, he thinks, and the

strength. Eat me, drink me, smell me. He himself has smiled to watch the worker ants pour forth, profuse, from their threshold, to follow a signal. A death scent sent across dirt, last licks. There's a brassy aroma that calls them. Even a tiger, dead in its darkness, meat eaten, ribcage empty hut. What do the hurrying worker ants know of him, climbing his final crumbs, his shreds: to them a feast. Between spasms of agony his mind continues to sprout vines and tendrils, fibrous analogies and assonances. Networks, he thinks, they savor me, eat me, drink me, have never seen me: minuscule insect lives whose trustfulness, though I slay them, makes me sigh. He feels how he reaches backward, fold beyond fold, in convolute dimension, unperceived. In the balloon of space, in the river of time, in ten or twenty further dimensions orthogonal each to other.

The cameras lean more impishly forward. They vibrate, they tremble, they dangle, they crane, of course it is sexual, like so much else. To their joy he is as photogenic as any movie icon. They adore his facial wrinkles, like the furrows in a landscape.

Sir. Sir. the back ones wave their arms, snap their fingers, trying desperately to get his attention before he croaks. Sir! All things are a flowing! Can you reveal the details of your will? Have you named a successor? He shakes his head somewhat angrily now. Where is his chief of staff to protect him? Where in hell are his secret service men? He can't see any uniforms. He is mischievously inclined to lift his nightie and show them his torso, bulbous as a termite's. The tubes bubble comfortably and he shakes his head. He can feel another convulsion of pain approaching, gathering force at a distance, a tsunami, sucking and rising.

Two of the women reporters in the back of the room are hum-
ming with their heads together. Nobody is allowed to light up
because of the oxygen. The two women duck silently out the
door, headed for the cafeteria, in rather obsessive need of a
coffee and a smoke; he gives them both the willies, turning to
protoplasm before their eyes, in that horrid green wrinkled
cotton gown, two or three brisk white hairs on his chest, he
reminds them of their fathers. The cafeteria, too, is desolate. A
cathedral of desolation.

He doesn't remember when he was born. He could calculate it
but he doesn't want to. He remembers creating Leviathan, an
ugly and violent monster covered with dung-colored scales,
during an experiment which taught him the sublimity of ugli-
ness. He remembers creating the sun, especially that thrilling
incandescent moment when light flashed out of it to fill the
darkness, and he remembers creating the moon. He remembers
the first plant growing out of his thumb, and the stream of birds
from his ear. He remembers Adam slipping out of his red hole,
such a soft surprise, and how he took him gently in his palms,
blew at him, and felt at that very moment as he waited for
Adam to awaken and gaze into his gaze, the drift into consciousness of a new sensation—his own importance—and how
he had always treasured new sensations. He remembers the
wars, those absorbing games with their swirling populations,
the minutiae of strategy and counterstrategy, the bulging bat-
tlegrounds and margins of forests, the individual flights of
heroism, the fine stink of a bloodsoaked field. He recalls Moses,
the pack animal, and that attractive boy David. Some of the
others blur. There was the charismatic lad, a genius at healing
and teaching others to heal, who ran into trouble with the

Romans and got himself executed. And the one who was crazy about writing and fighting, couldn't write himself yet dictated a splendid book from inspiration alone. He yawns operatically. He remembers pieces of music, pieces of architecture.

They all notice that he needs a shave. The jaws would be stubbly if you dared touch them. They have agreed that his voice is still an irresistible combination of thunder and honey, but that it already begins to be hollow, a wind blowing through an uninhabited mountain province. It is, they think, the voice of a celibate.

Sir! Sir! He nods wearily in that direction. It's a young man from one of the major Eastern newspapers.

Sir! Could you please distinguish between consubstantiation and transubstantiation?

The other reporters, not to mention all the cameramen, roll their eyes heavenward, thinking we can't all be from Harvard, and who gives a flying fuck. Little do they know of the early church, the desert fathers, the gnostic gospels and the Arian heresy, the Nicene Creed, the first crusade, the second through twelfth crusades, Pope Joan, the hundred years war, the thirty years war, the wars of the roses, the expulsion of the Moors, the holy inquisition, the wars of the Reformation, the warts of Cromwell, the eradication of witchcraft, or the syphilis of Nietzsche which is in fact responsible for their presence here today, and little care they; the empurpled sky outside the intensive care window reminds them how tired they are; it looks cold enough to snow out there although it seldom snows in this climate; at this hour of the afternoon everyone present is anticipating a beer a scotch a double bourbon a joint a snort a dinner with a friend a nap the drive home the subdivision the subway home the front door opening onto a warm living room a shower a new recording of Mozart's *C Minor Mass* the television cathode dimming and flaring the sports news and another beer and the dog.

The room is full of potted flowers. Streaked tulips violets azaleas calla lilies gaudy amaryllis some clothed in thin green tissue paper.

The room is full of chocolates. Mints cocoa creams raspberry creams mocha creams brazil nuts walnuts almonds truffles caramels, milk chocolates wrapped in red foil, green foil, silver foil, maraschino cherries afloat in translucent syrup, ruby seedy strawberries half hidden inside bittersweet chocolate vests. Mailed by well wishers. Some balloons cling tenderly to the ceiling, pale pink, lobelia and daffodil, sent by cripples, political prisoners, leaders of military regimes. Sent by pornographers and schoolchildren, gamblers and gunmen. They are among the many who entreat him to stay alive and want him to know they are praying for him, the balloons nuzzling each other electrostatically upon the ceiling signifying the celestial ascent of their desires. They send their prayers upward—like the balloons—for him, to him.

To pursue the new sensation, at whatever cost. To embrace pain if necessary in the quest for knowledge. Damn the torpedoes, full speed ahead. He remembers when the first female bit that idea. What did she do? Clever girl, she set about to produce expanded frontal lobes in her offspring, requiring a cranial volume which would scarcely squeeze through the maternal pelvis during labor. More knowledge meant bigger skulls, bigger skulls meant pain in childbirth. Warned, she dashed ahead, impetuous creature, he chuckled privately but proudly at her boldness. Like daughter like father, he too cultivates the intellectual impulsiveness which is so interesting a wrinkle in his polydimensional being. His convolute identity. He wishes he could trace these impulses to their mysterious source. Beyond the mistiness. He is trying to remember something, to remember something weighty yet shapeless, something he swallowed, back *there,* as he calls it. Back *there.* He almost has it. Like a sort of fish. Like a minnow thrashing its tail in the midst of a whale. But presently the agony comes on him, seizes him, an iridescent foam roaring up the beach.

The camera lenses observe his convulsions as the wave of tribulation drenches him, his reason temporarily canceled, his form increasingly fascinating. Will you look at that, say the photographers.

Meanwhile the two women reporters drink a cup of loathsome coffee in the deserted cafeteria. One of them takes out a pack of cigarettes and shakes it until the front ones slide up. Here, have a coffin nail. They inhale the toxic smoke, they exhale it, they suck luxuriously at their cigarettes, they are letting the ash grow longer, longer and then they knock it into the thick yellow saucer. They talk playfully, pleasantly, undistressed by the tacky chrome-and-plastic decor and the walls in need of repainting. Chloe likes Olivia. They work in the same newsroom.

We ought to get upstairs, says Chloe. He's supposed to represent goodness. You know. Feed the widow, clothe the orphan, love your neighbor.

That's the most ridiculous thing I ever heard, says Olivia.

Bloody right, says Chloe, who attended a good girls' school where they did Classics, History, and Bible in the old-fashioned, edifying way designed to help the ruling classes exude the confidence required by their position. Ridiculing the stuffiness of their education is one of the signs of that confidence. But there it is, she adds, however absurd the invention.

Olivia counters: "In the tabernacle it is metamorphosed as a boxful of nothing that no one would miss. The trick of the 'omnipotent.' The voice saying 'I-am-who-I-say-I-am.'" Who am I quoting?

Fortunately, yawns Chloe, he can't die, he's only temporarily indisposed, it's just another media occasion, we needn't be in such a stew.

Who's this we, white girl, says Olivia.

But my God, says Chloe, did you see how bloated he looked there. He looked pregnant. Perhaps he's having a baby instead of a cancer.

Olivia inadvertently laughs, dribbling coffee and making a rude noise. O right, she says after swallowing. Pregnant. What a riot. God in labor. Believe that? She punches Chloe on the shoulder.

I believe because it is absurd, says Chloe, showing off her excellent education. Well, burn my bush, says Olivia.

A Prayer to the Shekhinah

*For I will turn their mourning into joy, and I will
comfort them, and make them rejoice from their
sorrow.*
JEREMIAH 31:13

*It will certainly come. . . .
When it comes, everyone will see it. . . .
Sometimes I disguise myself as a dead woman. . . .
With endless yearning
I breathe upon these dead ones here
That they may live.*
DAHLIA RAVIKOVICH

Come be our mother   we are your young ones
Come be our bride   we are your lover
Come be our dwelling   we are your inhabitants
Come be our game   we are your players
Come be our punishment   we are your sinners
Come be our ocean   we are your swimmers
Come be our victory   we are your army
Come be our laughter   we are your story
Come be our Shekhinah   we are your glory
We believe that you live
Though you delay   we believe you will certainly come

When the transformation happens as it must
When we remember

When she wakes from her long repose in us
When she wipes the nightmare
Of history from her eyes
When she returns from exile
When she utters her voice in the streets
In the opening of the gates
How long, you simple ones, will you
Love simplicity, and the scorners delight
In their scorning, and fools hate knowledge
When she enters the modern world
When she crosses the land
Shaking her breasts and hips
With timbrels and with dances
Magnified and sanctified
Exalted and honored
Blessed and glorified
When she causes tyranny
To vanish
When she and he meet
When they behold each other face to face
When they become naked and not ashamed
On that day will our God be One
And their name One

Shekhinah bless us and keep us
Shekhinah shine your face on us
Shekhinah turn your countenance
To us and give us peace

Further Reading

◈ *Some Further Reading* ◈

Alter, Robert. *The Art of Biblical Narrative*. New York: Basic Books, 1981.

Alter, Robert, and Frank Kermode, eds. *The Literary Guide to the Bible*. Cambridge, Mass.: Harvard University Press, 1987.

Armstrong, Karen. *A History of God*. New York: Alfred A. Knopf, 1994.

Bloom, Harold, ed. *The Bible: Modern Critical Views*. New York: Chelsea House, 1987.

Bal, Mieke. *Death & Dissymetry: The Politics of Coherence in the Book of Judges*. Chicago: University of Chicago Press, 1988.

Boyarin, Daniel. *Carnal Israel: Reading Sex in Talmudic Culture*. Berkeley: University of California Press, 1993.

Buber, Martin. "Job." In *The Bible: Modern Critical Views*, ed. Bloom.

———. *I and Thou*. Trans. Ronald Gregor Smith. New York: Scribners, 1958.

———. *Moses, the Revelation and the Covenant*. New York: Harper & Brothers, 1958.

Bruns, Gerald R. "Midrash and Allegory." In *The Literary Guide to the Bible*, ed. Alter and Kermode.

Callaway, Mary. *Sing, O Barren One: A Study in Comparative Midrash*. Atlanta: Scholars Press, 1986.

Christ, Carol, and Judith Plaskow. *Womanspirit Rising: A Feminist Reader in Religion*. San Francisco: Harper & Row, 1979.

Cross, Frank. *Canaanite Myth and Hebrew Epic*. Cambridge, Mass.: Harvard University Press, 1973.

Douglas, Mary. *Purity and Danger*. Westport, Conn.: Praeger, 1966.

Eliade, Mircea, editor in chief. *The Encyclopedia of Religion*. New York: Collier Macmillan, 1987.

Encyclopedia Judaica. 16 vols. Jerusalem: Kater Publishing House, 1972.

Frazer, James. *The Golden Bough, a Study in Magic and Religion*. New York: St. Martin's Press, 1990.

Friedman, Richard Eliot. *Who Wrote the Bible?* San Francisco: Harper & Row, 1987.

Freud, Sigmund. *Moses and Monotheism*. Trans. Katherine Jones. New York: Vintage, 1967.

Frymer-Kensky, Tikva. *In the Wake of the Goddesses: Women, Culture, and the Biblical Transformation of Pagan Myth*. New York: The Free Press, 1992.

Ginsberg, Louis. *The Legends of the Jews*. Trans. Henrietta Szold. 7 vols. Jewish Publication Society, 1909–1966.

Grahn, Judy. *Blood, Bread, and Roses: How Menstruation Created the World*. Boston: Beacon Press, 1993.

Hartman, Geoffrey, and Sanford Budick, eds. *Midrash and Literature*. New Haven: Yale University Press, 1986.

Heidel, Alexander. *The Babylonian Genesis: The Story of Creation*. Chicago: University of Chicago Press, 1951.

Heschel, Susannah, ed. *On Being a Jewish Feminist*. New York: Schocken 1983.

Kaye/Kantrowitz, Melanie, and Irena Klepfisz, eds. *The Tribe of Dina: a Jewish Woman's Anthology*. Boston: Beacon Press, 1989.

Knopp, Josephine Zadovsky. *The Trial of Judaism in Contemporary Jewish Writing*. Urbana: University of Illinois Press, 1975.

Kristeva, Julia. *Powers of Horror: an Essay on Abjection*. Trans. Leon S. Roudiez. New York: Columbia University Press, 1982.

Layton, Anson. *Arguing with God: A Jewish Tradition*. Northvale, N.J. and London: J. Aronson, 1990.

Lerner, Gerda. *The Creation of Patriarchy*. New York: Oxford University Press, 1986.

Matt, Daniel Chanan, trans. and intro. *Zohar—the Book of Enlightenment*. Preface by Arthur Green. Ramsey, N.J.: Paulist Press, 1983.

Mathers, S. L. *The Kabbalah Unveiled*. London: Routledge and Kegan Paul, 1957.

Metzger, Deena. *What Dinah Thought*. New York: Viking, 1989.

Mitchell, Stephen, trans. and intro. *The Book of Job*. New York: Harper & Row, 1992.

Monaghan, Patricia. *The Book of Goddesses and Heroines*. New York: Dutton, 1981.

Ozick, Cynthia. "Ruth." In *Congregation*, ed. Rosenberg.

Pardes, Ilana. *Countertraditions in the Bible: A Feminist Approach*. Cambridge, Mass.: Harvard University Press, 1992.

Patai, Raphael. *The Hebrew Goddess*. New York: Avon, 1978.

Plaskow, Judith. *Standing Again at Sinai*. San Francisco: Harper & Row, 1990.

Rosenberg, David, ed. *Congregation: Contemporary Writers Read the Jewish Bible*. San Diego: Harcourt Brace, 1987.

Scholem, Gershom. *On the Kabbalah and Its Symbolism.* Trans. Ralph Mannheim. New York: Schocken, 1965.

Segal, Lore. "II Samuel." in *Congregation*, ed. Rosenberg.

Stone, Merlin. *When God Was a Woman.* San Diego: Harcourt Brace, 1976.

Teubal, Savina J. *Sarah the Priestess: The First Matriarch of Genesis.* Athens, Ohio: Swallow Press, 1984.

Trible, Phyllis. *God and the Rhetoric of Sexuality.* Philadelphia: Fortress Press, 1978.

Walker, Barbara G. *The Women's Encyclopedia of Myths and Secrets.* San Francisco: Harper & Row, 1983.

Walzer, Michael. *Exodus and Revolution.* New York: Basic Books, 1985.